BAUDELAIRE AND FREUD

Leo Bersani

Baudelaire and Freud

University of California Press

Berkeley · Los Angeles · London

Other books by Leo Bersani

Marcel Proust: The Fictions of Life and of Art
*Balzac to Beckett: Center and Circumference in French
    Fiction*
*A Future for Astyanax: Character and Desire in
    Literature*

University of California Press
Berkeley and Los Angeles, California

University of California Press, Ltd.
London, England

ISBN 0–520–03402–3
Library of Congress Catalog Card Number: 76–55562
Printed in the United States of America
Designed by Hal Hershey

1 2 3 4 5 6 7 8 9

Contents

For Eléonore Zimmermann

Introduction

Baudelaire's work can be viewed as an exemplary drama in our culture. It illustrates in striking fashion both the persistence and the subversion of idealistic vision in modern literature. Baudelaire continuously returns to categories discredited by the experiences evoked in his most original writing. For example, he has frequently been discussed in terms of what he himself calls, in "Mon Coeur mis à nu," "two postulations" in human nature: "There are in every man, at every moment, two simultaneous postulations, one toward God, the other toward Satan. The invocation to God, or spirituality, is a desire to climb higher; Satan's invocation, or animality, is a delight in descent."[1] Baudelaire's work can indeed be read as a dramatic confirmation of this traditional dualism be-

1. Charles Baudelaire, *Oeuvres complètes,* ed. Y.-G. Le Dantec and Claude Pichois (Paris, 1961), p. 1277. All quotations from Baudelaire, unless otherwise indicated, will be from this Pléiade edition, and page references will be given in the text. All prose translations are my own. For quotations from *Les Fleurs du mal,* the French is indispensable; as a convenience to readers, I give in the footnotes Francis Scarfe's "plain prose translations," as he calls them, of Baudelaire's verse in *Baudelaire* (Baltimore: Penguin Books, 1961). A warning: Scarfe presents the poems in a blend of chronological sequence and grouping by "cycles," thereby largely neglecting the order of both the 1857 and 1861 editions. I am very grateful to Francis Scarfe for his permission to use these translations.

tween spirit and flesh, between aspirations toward purity and an equally intense appetite for self-degradation or "evil." But such a reading involves an uncritical fidelity to Baudelaire's least original version of a certain mobility in his being and in his poetry. The two "postulations"—as well as the entire moral and religious vocabulary to which they give rise in Baudelaire—can in fact be thought of as an escape from the anxieties produced by the Baudelairean discovery of psychic mobility, of unanchored identity.

Baudelaire's notion of a double postulation in human nature belongs to a system of vertical transcendence. It is the psychological aspect of a more general structuring of experience in terms of high and low, spirit and matter, reality and appearance, truth and error. In literature, we have long been familiar with the tensions produced by an opposition between certain realities presumed to be "given" and a heroic effort to go beyond the limits of a centered, socially defined, time-bound self. But the antagonism between social reality and individual aspiration is itself one of the dualities formulated by the idealistic imagination. This is not to say that the opposition doesn't exist, or even that it can't serve as a basis for revolutionary social action. But if the type of heroic individuality most familiar to us has frequently been doomed to a romantic impotence, it may be because such transcendental yearnings obliquely express a cultural compulsion regarding coherent structures and intelligible limits. One does, however, find in modern literature—roughly from Baudelaire and Lautréamont to some contemporary theatrical experiments—a form of disruptive desire infinitely more concrete in its psychic effects and social implications than a rebellious idealistic vision. I'm thinking of attempts to dismiss defined structures of the self and of society which, however, do not include any faith or even interest in a "higher" or "truer" self, or in fact any transcendent reality at all "beyond" the known self. Visionary literature, even when it proclaims the failure of visionary desires, clings to the belief that the vision was *of something*. We find a quite different phenomenon in what I take to be the most radical modern writing. As an alternative to both the socially defined self and the transcendent (or free or universal) self, literature has also celebrated marginal or partial selves, or, to put it in another way, a disseminated, scattered self which resists all efforts to make a unifying structure of fragmented desire. At the extreme, there would be no privileged "place" which the self could return to as a structuring center. What would ordinarily have been thought of as psychic peripheries appear no longer to be referring to fixed centers; there are only provisional, constantly shifting centers for a self which would seem to be floating among random images collected from anywhere.[2]

2. This paragraph takes up some of the introductory comments in my recent book *A Future for Astyanax / Character and Desire in Literature* (Boston and Toronto: Little, Brown, 1976). In the present study, I return to some of the issues raised in that book. I consider them in a more consistently Freudian framework; my aim has been to test the viability of a highly speculative psychoanalytic vocabulary in what is a close reading of a single author. I am aware that some of my interpretations will strike very good readers of Baudelaire as outrageous violations of his work. I would therefore like to

Baudelaire's work gives us images of this psychic fragmentation at the same time that it documents a determined resistance to all such ontological floating. This tension accounts for much of the interest of Baudelaire. Like Freud, he can be located at that critical moment in our culture's history when an idealistic view of the self and of the universe is being simultaneously held onto and discredited by a psychology (if the word still applies) of the fragmented and the discontinuous. Now we might have considered more radical versions of a fragmented, mobile self than those we will find in Baudelaire. Psychic fragmentation, self-dissemination, affective discontinuity and partial selves have become ideological tenets of much contemporary thought. There is, however, good reason to be skeptical about the practical value of recent blueprints for a revolution of consciousness, and the evident difficulty in making even the first steps in such a

---

say at the outset that, however uncompromisingly dogmatic much of what follows may sound, this book is intended as an experimental working out of a hypothesis concerning a particular form of intertextuality (relations between literary and psychoanalytic texts). And in order to provide that hypothesis with the most favorable testing conditions, I have deliberately ignored some other critical approaches which would make this study perhaps more reasonable (and palatable), but which would also reduce the value of the experiment. The traditionally liberal approach to literature is, as we should all know by now, far from being nondogmatic; the commitment to a kind of noncommitment in the area of critical theory is itself ideologically loaded. Therefore, a surely desirable generosity toward one set of hypotheses perhaps requires—if only provisionally—an apparent inhospitality toward other approaches which, in the case of Baudelaire at any rate, have certainly had their say.

revolution suggests the usefulness of stepping back and exploring more carefully and more coolly our potentialities for both rigidity and change. In the same way that the ambivalences and even contradictions of Freud make it more instructive to explore *his* thought rather than the thought of Ronald Laing, it is more profitable to study a crisis in subjectivity in Baudelaire than in the programmatic subversion of the subject in Alain Robbe-Grillet. A complex and even confused resistance to the indeterminacy of being that is dramatized in Baudelaire's greatest poems will permit us to examine the phenomenon of problematic identity in ways not allowed for by the essentially pastoral, frequently simplistic versions of the same phenomenon in contemporary writing.

Freudian texts, and recent French interpretations of Freud, will be important in my reading of Baudelaire. What is the relevance of Freudian theory to literary criticism? The question has been endlessly argued—without, I feel, many interesting results. On the whole, psychoanalytically oriented criticism has been reductive in two respects: it interprets literature as a system of sexual symbolism, and, correlatively with this, it re-places the writer within the infantile sexual organization presumably indicated by his preferred symbols. Most psychoanalytic studies of literature have used the notion of fantasy as a means of *im*mobilizing the writer (and the problem is not only a literary or even an artistic one) in certain fixed desires or sexual scenarios. From this perspective, Freudian theory essentially buttresses a normative view of psycho-sexual growth; it encourages us to think in terms of "lower" and "higher" stages of development by emphasizing both the biological necessity and the desirability of a definite scheme of human growth. Freudianism thus becomes a technique for transforming the experimental play of fantasy into a rigidly structured self.

But the relevance of Freudian theory to literature has little to do with either symbol hunting or the determination of the stage of sexual development in childhood—oral, anal, or phallic—at which a writer may be "fixated." A psychoanalytic theory of fantasy can be most profitably brought into analyses of literary texts not in terms of specific sexual content, but rather in terms of the mobility of fantasy, of its potential for explosive displacements. We will be operating on the fundamental Freudian assumption that no text is ever fully present to itself. There is a fantasmatic supplement, an absent extension of itself which a text never explicitly articulates but incessantly refers to, which it makes imperative only, as it were, by the high visibility of significant lacks. And what is lacking is not a fixed symbolic equivalence which, once revealed, would tell us what the text is "really saying." A frankly compulsive attention to specific texts will propel us away from these same texts into a fascination with other texts having the same potential for both fixing and scattering our attention. These other texts will be both the unexpressed Baudelairean fantasies and the speculative psychoanalytic texts thanks to which we will have uncovered these fantasies but which are themselves problematic textual surfaces. All these absent texts will be treated as supplementary disruptive movements which simultaneously bring a certain coherence to the given literary text and accelerate its disruptive interpretive mobility. (The modifications of Freudian theory which I will be proposing, especially in the discussions of masochism and the superego in the second half of this study, are themselves vulnerable to explosive contacts with still other texts not considered here.)

There is, it's true, ample justification for reductive psychoanalytic interpretation in Freud himself. But it is also possible to find in Freud the basis of a theory of fantasy as a phenomenon of psychic deconstruction. Deconstruction and mobility: these are the mental processes in which we discover that self-scattering which is the principal feature of Baudelairean desire. This discovery is important for both esthetics and psychological theory. It implies a radical questioning of traditional assumptions about the nature and stability of structuring processes in art and, more generally, in the self. Freudian theory serves the most constraining cultural enterprises in some of its statements about the history of our desiring fantasies; but it also outlines the operations of fantasy in ways which explode its own narrow views of the "natural" shapes and rhythms of desire and fantasy. A similar tension can be found in Baudelaire: between the rhythms of mobile fantasy and the rigidity of a self frozen in an obscurantist opposition between God and Satan, between spirit and flesh.

1
Artists in Love

Love is the desire to prostitute oneself.
. . . .
What is art? Prostitution. (1247)

What is love?
The need to go outside oneself.
Man is an adoring animal.
To adore is to sacrifice oneself and to prostitute oneself.
Thus all love is prostitution.

The most prostituted being is the Supreme Being, God Himself,
since for every individual he is the friend above all others, since he
is the common, inexhaustible reservoir of love. (1286–87)

A woman is hungry and she wants to eat. Thirsty and she wants to
drink.
She is in heat and she wants to be screwed.
What admirable qualities!
Woman is *natural,* that is to say abominable. (1272)

The more man cultivates the arts, the less he can get a hard-on.
A more and more apparent divorce takes place between the spirit
and the brute.
Only the brute has no trouble getting a hard-on, and screwing is
the lyricism of the masses.

To screw is to aspire to enter into another person, and the artist
never goes outside himself. (1295–96)

Art, love, prostitution, impotence, androgyny, and
divinity: Baudelaire frequently seems to be proposing

a fundamental identity among all these terms. In the aphoristic prose of the *Journaux intimes,* he makes a strikingly unstable effort to locate the sexuality of art. From the enigmatic pronouncements just quoted, we can, however, infer a kind of fantasy-logic. Art resembles love in that both the lover and the artist go outside themselves; they lose themselves in others. This is not merely poetic empathy. Baudelaire is anxious to describe something more radical than a sympathetic projection into other people's lives. And his feelings about the prostitution of self inherent in love and art vary wildly. In the prose poem "Les Foules," Baudelaire praises "that ineffable orgy, that holy prostitution of the soul which, in an act of poetry and charity, gives itself entirely to the unexpected and to the unknown" (244). But in "Le *Confiteor* de l'Artiste" (also from the *Petits Poèmes en prose),* the very energy of an ecstatic loss or drowning of the self in "the immensity of the sky and the sea" at the end of an autumnal afternoon "creates a malaise and a positive suffering. My excessively taut nerves now transmit only screaming and painful vibrations" (232). Finally, in the passages quoted a moment ago from the *Journaux intimes,* the artist's availability to others is linked to the "abominable naturalness" of women. Both love and art are natural activities ("Man is an adoring animal"), and, with his usual ambivalence toward the idea of nature, Baudelaire characterizes the lover's and the artist's desires to prostitute themselves as both a holy and degrading openness. What exactly is the nature of this openness?

In his essay on Constantin Guys, "Le Peintre de la

vie moderne," Baudelaire tells the story of a friend—
now "a famous painter"—who, as a child, would
watch his father getting dressed and "contemplate,
with both dazed astonishment and joy, the muscles
of his arms, the gradations of his skin coloring tinged
with pink and yellow, and the bluish network of his
veins." Baudelaire suggests that the child's essentially
artistic contemplation of the world is the equivalent
of a violent appropriation of the self by forms alien to
it: "The spectacle of external life was already filling
him with respect and taking hold of his mind [Le
tableau de la vie extérieure le pénétrait déjà de respect
et s'emparait de son cerveau]. Form already obsessed
him and possessed him." Before anything new, the
child's (and the artist's) gaze is "fixed" and expresses
an "animal-like ecstasy [l'oeil fixe et animalement
extatique]." The self is suddenly possessed, filled up,
even shaken by a scene from the world. "I will venture
further; I maintain that inspiration is related to *cerebral
congestion,* and that every sublime thought is accompanied by a nervous shock or jolt [une secousse
nerveuse], which varies in strength and which rever-
berates even in the cerebellum" (1159).

Artistic attention produces ecstasy and dissipates
the self's integrity. "To go outside oneself" is equivalent to allowing the self to be penetrated, to having it
invaded, congested, and shattered by the objects of its
attention. Now the idea of the artist's prostitution
covers two radically different experiences in Baudelaire. On the one hand, the artist-prostitute's "ineffable orgy" of openness to the world corresponds,
as we shall see in the second half of this study, to a

narcissistic appropriation of the world. The self is "lost" only to be relocated everywhere. In part, the description of Constantin Guys as "homme des foules" designates prostitution as a narcissistic strategy. "To be away from home, and yet to feel everywhere at home; to see the world, to be at the center of the world and remain hidden from the world, these are some of the lesser pleasures of those independent, passionate, impartial spirits who can be described only awkwardly in language. The observer is a *prince* who enjoys being incognito everywhere." When this observer rushes into the crowd, it is, as in Poe's story "The Man of the Crowd," in order to pursue a stranger who seems to be his double; Poe's convalescent hero, evoked by Baudelaire in "Le Peintre de la vie moderne," is fascinated by a man who reproduces his own passionate interest in crowds (1160, 1158). But Baudelaire also speaks, in the essay on Guys, of the artist being shattered by otherness. He is penetrated, congested, and shaken by the heterogeneity of "the spectacle of external life." The artist is excited *by and into* alien images. There is then the possibility that by prostituting himself, the artist, like the lover, will be "sacrificing" himself—or, more exactly, sacrificing a certain wholeness or integrity for the sake of those pleasurable nervous shocks which accompany the release of desiring energies by scenes from external life.

In the *Journaux intimes,* the shattering of the artist's integrity is also seen as a momentous sexual event. In order to be possessed by alien images, the artist must open himself in a way which Baudelaire immediately

associates with feminine sexuality. Psychic penetrability is fantasized as sexual penetrability, and in glorify-
ing "the cult of images" as "my great, my unique, my
primary passion," Baudelaire is also confessing a passion which may change him into a woman (1295).
Michel Butor has taken the opposite position, main-
taining that images of masculine sexuality are linked to
the fact of being a poet for Baudelaire. But this connection has less to do with the poet's intrinsic nature than
with the will necessary for composition, and especially
for publication. It is true, as Butor says, that Baudelaire
associates will with virility, but the loss of virility cannot be reduced to a loss of will. Instead, will is a kind of
secondary virility which struggles against a much
more fundamental devirilization. For Butor, the decision of Baudelaire's family in 1844 to appoint a legal
guardian who would dole out his inheritance to him
for the rest of his life "devirilized" Baudelaire. [1] But the
passages we are looking at from the *Journaux intimes*
suggest that the very nature of poetic inspiration is
enough to transform the poet from a man into a
woman. The "abominable" feature of women is that
they are "natural," and the examples of their closeness
to nature all have to do with their appetite to absorb
(food, drink, and the penis). They would seem to be
characterized by an animal ecstasy very much like that
ecstatic openness which, in "Le Peintre de la vie moderne," Baudelaire finds in children and in artists.

The paradoxical final consequence of this line of
(fantasy) reasoning is that the very sexuality of art de-

1. *Histoire extraordinaire / Essai sur un rêve de Baudelaire* (Paris,
1961), pp. 40–42.

sexualizes the artist. The last passage from the *Journaux intimes* quoted at the beginning of this chapter is ambiguous in this respect. "The more man cultivates the arts, the less he can get a hard-on." But the reasons which Baudelaire gives for this sexual debilitation seem to go against what we have just been saying. Art would now seem to belong to the domain of the spiritual; the artist gradually loses contact with his bodily appetites because of a divorce between his flesh and his spirit. The idea of going outside oneself reappears in this passage, but now it is connected with the antithesis of artistic activity, with carnal appetites. Sex, brutishness, the absence of art, and going outside oneself all belong together; on the other side, there is impotence, spirituality, art, and a permanent self-containment (the artist never leaves himself).

But even here the antithesis is somewhat qualified by the suggestion that sexual energy may not be the opposite of art, but the only version of art which the lower classes are capable of producing. Sex *is* art, but art takes the form of sex only in the masses: "Screwing is the lyricism of the masses." The "opposition" between the activities of the flesh and those of the spirit may turn out to be a continuous scale of expression for a single impulse. Furthermore, the assertion of the artist's self-protective immobility is in such profound contradiction not only with other theoretical statements, but also—as we shall be seeing at some length—with so much of Baudelaire's poetry, that we may suspect it to be a defense against Baudelaire's most powerfully felt experience of art. In "Le Peintre de la vie moderne," Baudelaire significantly hesitates to call

Guys a dandy because of the very quality which accounts for his being an artist: his "insatiable passion"
to see and to feel, to lose himself in crowds ("Sa passion et sa profession, c'est d'*épouser la foule*"). It is by
his inability to remain "insensitive" (or self-contained)
that Guys "detaches himself violently from dandyism" (1160).[2] We may therefore conclude that behind the explicit statement from the *Journaux* which
we have just considered, there is a hidden assertion: the
sexual explosiveness of artistic activity (rather than its
"spirituality") renders the artist impotent. The constant in Baudelaire's thought would be the idea of a
connection between art and the loss of virility. At
times, it is the sublimity of art which accounts for this
loss; at other times—and, I think, much more
interestingly—the artist loses his virile identity *through*
an obscene openness to external reality which makes
him an artist but which also makes him—a woman.[3]

2. Speaking of the same passage, Sartre writes: ". . . it is clear
that dandyism represents a higher ideal than poetry"; it is Baudelaire's "sterile wish" for something beyond poetry (Jean-Paul
Sartre, *Baudelaire* [Paris: Gallimard, 1947] pp. 183, 196).
3. Baudelaire's attitude toward the artist's dual sexuality is not
always negative. In *Les Paradis artificiels,* he speaks of "a delicate
skin, a distinguished accent, a kind of androgynous quality" ac-
quired by men raised principally by women ("L'homme qui, dès
le commencement, a été longtemps baigné dans la molle atmos-
phère de la femme"). Without these qualities, ". . . the roughest
and most virile genius remains, as far as artistic perfection is concerned, an incomplete being" (444–45). Butor sees the *mundus
muliebris* as the "necessary theater" in which the artist, by an act of
will, conquers his virility—and his artistic powers. The devirilized
male artist who desires women is, as Butor nicely concludes, a les-
bian, and lesbians for Baudelaire are "the very symbol of the ap-
prentice poet, of the poet who has not yet published" *(Histoire extraordinaire,* pp. 79, 85–86).

The artist is intrinsically an unanchored self. The energy with which he penetrates the world (or is penetrated by the world) sets him afloat among alien forms of being. And, because they repeat the poet's exceptional openness, God and lovers similarly partake of the exhilarating risks of problematic being. In love and in art, identity floats. Its wholeness can be shattered, as we have begun to see, in various ways. The self may be invaded by scenes from the world to the point of not being able to maintain any distance from them, to the point of being entirely absorbed in them. Psychic identity is also dissipated by the very force with which it is projected toward others in the same way that the orgasm dissipates the intensity of our sexual desire for others. Or, conversely, consciousness adopts an ecstatic passivity before the "spectacle of external life," a passivity which in itself transforms the poet into a woman. The *Journaux intimes* are thus exceptionally suggestive about the relation between poetic production and sexuality. For Baudelaire, the esthetic imagination is inseparable from erotic intensities and shifting sexual identities. His work is, as a result, an extraordinarily rich document about both the nature of sensual pleasure in poetic activity and the psychic dislocations implicit in poetic (erotic) fantasy.

2
Architectural Secrets

"The only praise I earnestly seek for this book is for people to recognize that it is not merely an album and that it has a beginning and an end."[1] Baudelaire's emphasis on the coherent wholeness of *Les Fleurs du mal* would seem to justify critical efforts to describe that "secret architecture" to which Barbey d'Aurevilly referred in his 1857 essay on Baudelaire. The architectural metaphor is both crucial and ambiguous. On the one hand, it seems clear that Baudelaire always thought of his poems as constituting a single unified work. The thirty-five poems which he added to the 1857 edition of *Les Fleurs du mal* for the 1861 edition modify the content of the work without changing the poet's architectural intention. New poems enter into a preexistent structure; presumably, they don't disrupt an already given structural completeness. *Les Fleurs du mal* is similar to *A la Recherche du temps perdu* in this respect: both works appear to be governed by the esthetic myth of nontransforming additions. New passages, to take up an image used by Proust himself in *Le Temps retrouvé,* are simply sewn into the book's fabric. There is already a beginning and an ending, an

1. Letter to Alfred de Vigny, in *Correspondance Générale de Charles Baudelaire,* ed. Jacques Crépet, 6 vols. (Paris: Louis Conard, 1947–53), 4:9.

architectural enclosure which will contain (both hold and limit the effectiveness of) what is new. Instead of a literary work being produced by composition, we would have a work preceding and fundamentally unaffected by compositional activities.[2]

But Proust also saw the breakdown of an esthetic of completeness in nineteenth-century art. In *La Prisonnière,* the narrator speaks ambivalently of "the literary miscarriages of [the century's] greatest writers," of how their works "participate in the quality of being—albeit marvelously—always incomplete." At the same time, Proust notes a kind of retrospective compulsion to unity on the part of these same writers, although he himself hesitates between two views of the unity of *La Comédie humaine* and of Wagner's tetralogy. Is that unity (which has been "unaware of itself, therefore vital and not logical") intrinsic to the works themselves? Or is the completeness of these works merely an inventive idea *about* each work, "a novel beauty" derived from the artist's self-contemplation and which is "exterior and superior to

---

2. One can of course maintain that the additions, deletions, and rearrangements of 1861 change the work's "moral argument." But I'm interested in the notion of completeness itself, and I don't wish to make a case for *any* meaning in Baudelaire's poetry which would merely assume the work's architectural stability. Those interested in critical attempts to articulate the "secret architecture" of *Les Fleurs du mal* might begin with Albert Feuillerat, *L'Architecture des "Fleurs du mal"* in *Studies by Members of the French Department of Yale University* (New Haven, 1941); L. F. Benedetto, *L'Architecture des "Fleurs du mal"* in *Zeitschrift für französische Sprache und Literatur,* vol. 39 (1912); and Marcel A. Ruff, *Baudelaire* (Paris, 1966), pp. 103–21.

the work itself, imposing upon it retrospectively a unity, a greatness which it does not possess?" It is as if Proust were simultaneously convinced of the factitious nature of such unities and nostalgic for a traditional esthetic which could speak of unity and completeness not as critical imperatives about art but as qualities inherent in authentic art. (Thus the Proustian narrator writes that Michelet's prefaces to the *Histoire de France* and the *Histoire de la Révolution*— "prefaces, that is to say pages written after the books themselves"—are where "the greatest beauties in Michelet are found." A discredited critical myth is promoted—or degraded?—to the status of esthetic form.[3])

The subversion of unity and completeness both as demonstrable attributes of works of art and as critical tenets is familiar to us in forms much more radical than those imagined by Proust. In our century an esthetic of *in*completion and fragmentariness has corresponded to a questioning of general cultural assumptions about the nature of the self and the "shapes" of human experience. But in the artists mentioned by Proust, as well as in Baudelaire and in Proust himself, the finished architectural quality of art is called into question partly as a result of the very emphasis given to that quality. Unity is betrayed as problematic by virtue of its having become so programmatic.

Baudelaire's insistence on the coherent wholeness of

3. Marcel Proust, *A la Recherche du temps perdu,* ed. Pierre Clarac and André Ferré, 3 vols. (Paris: Gallimard, 1954), 3:160–61. I discuss the passage from *La Prisonnière* in greater detail in *Balzac to Beckett* (New York: Oxford University Press, 1970), pp. 193–97.

his book—on its having a real beginning and real ending—suggests a neatly thematic view of *Les Fleurs du mal*. The poems would have a traceable significance, and the order in which they appear would correspond to different stages of a drama working toward a dénouement. Indeed, many critics have sought to articulate those stages. For traditional Baudelairean criticism, *Les Fleurs du mal* tells a story of great spiritual intensity, of a struggle between the "two postulations," between the satanic and the godly in man, or, to use the title of the book's first section, between "spleen and ideal." Thematic enclosures, however, immobilize the work's significance; they put an end to the circulation of its meanings. There is another "secret architecture" in *Les Fleurs du mal,* one which both explains the need for and subverts a stabilizing thematic architecture. The work is organized along the lines of an approach to, and then a retreat from, a conception of desire which, had it been fully triumphant, might have precluded any possibility of architectural organization. Order would be nonarchitectural; or, at the very least, the poet would invite us to conceive of architectural orders as made of movable parts.

Baudelaire has an exceptionally acute sense of the congeniality of modern art to a fracturing of both inner and outer realities. His response to the problematic status of art in the nineteenth century is in part what might be called a transcendental escapism; but he also tries to elucidate a viable esthetic from those very conditions of modern life which he rightly sees as a major threat to the moral, psychological, and structural securities of traditional art. *"The beautiful is always bizarre"*—and the bizarre is constituted by a particularity so radical as to resist any generalizing enterprise. The particular is not necessarily a source of the general. It is as if a kind of exhilarating meaninglessness in the fragmented, madly diversified scenes of modern life led Baudelaire to the notion of a particularity which, as it were, goes nowhere, which is not a "part" of anything. "Astonishment, which is one of the great pleasures [jouissances] caused by art and literature," is the result of such an extreme variety in artistic effects that each one of them seems entirely new, unrepeatable ("Exposition universelle de 1855," 956). But Baudelaire also feels the compulsion to *complete* these impressions of modern art. In "De l'Idéal et du Modèle" (from the "Salon de 1846"), Baudelaire remarks that ". . . nothing in nature is absolute, or even complete; I see only individuals." But in a footnote to this sentence, he adds: "Nothing absolute:—thus, the ideal of the compass is the worst of stupidities;—neither is there anything complete:—thus it is necessary to complete everything, and to rediscover each ideal" (913). Baudelaire defeats the radical nature of his own modernism by insisting on its being complemented by an esthetic which it has already replaced. "Modernity," he writes in "Le Peintre de la vie moderne," "is the transitory, the fugitive, the contingent; it is half of art, and the other half is the eternal and the immutable" (1163). Thus the bizarre, the accidental, the fragmentary, instead of having any finality in art (or in the rest of life), are merely fallen modes of being. Baudelaire combines an esthetic of modernism with a hatred of modern life, and one result of this is an attempt to justify the modernist esthetic by placing it within a "larger" view of art which almost cancels it out.

Les Fleurs du mal is *about* meaning. In his most original poems, Baudelaire is testing the viability of certain ways of creating sense which would make sense irreducible to theme. Sense would, so to speak, always be on the move; it would be inseparable from mobile fantasies. But, because of Baudelaire's ambivalent feelings about this disruptive discovery, the poems which dismiss an architectural thematics of literature are themselves enclosed within a structure of what might be called a stabilizing suspicion. There is a shifting between types of meaning in *Les Fleurs du mal* which in itself constitutes an important meaning in the work. But it is one which has an extremely ambiguous status, for, at every step in the work, it implicitly refers us to the *other* sense-making mode from which it is in flight. Thus, to follow the order of poems in *Les Fleurs du mal* may help us to see just how seriously that order is threatened. And the threat can't be located at any one moment in the volume, or at any one period of Baudelaire's life. A disruptive mobility of fantasy and the immobilization of desire are scattered throughout both the work and the life (with, of course, certain "passages" in both where pressures, so to speak, accumulate more thickly). For example, "Les Bijoux" and "A Celle qui est trop gaie" precede "Le Beau navire" and "L'Invitation au voyage" in the 1857 edition—although the first two poems can be read as a refusal of the indeterminacy of being with which Baudelaire plays in "L'Invitation" and "Le Beau navire." Also, "Les Bijoux" (1842) was written several years before "Le

Beau navire" (probably 1854) and "L'Invitation au voyage" (1848 according to Marcel Ruff, 1854 according to Antoine Adam). *Les Fleurs du mal* has, as Baudelaire wished it to have, "a beginning and an end," but what is begun and what is ended is an experiment that might have resulted in a universe of meaning in which beginnings and endings would be irrelevant. To be faithful to the well-worn notion of a "secret architecture" in *Les Fleurs du mal* may therefore—contrary to the usual aim of fidelity to that notion in criticism—actually mean trying to delineate the process by which an apparent architectural center perversely works against all architectural solidity.

3
Elevations and Ennui

Les Fleurs du mal opens with some of Baudelaire's most famous, and least interesting, poems: "Bénédiction," "L'Albatros," "Elévation," and "Les Phares." It is here that Baudelaire expresses most unambiguously an idealistic view of the poet which, on the whole, *Les Fleurs du mal* simply dismisses. These early poems pick up the most familiar romantic version of that view. The poet is "exiled" on earth; other men misunderstand and mistreat him; his only "home" is "the luminous and serene fields" high above the "morbid miasmas" of earthly existence. The poet, like the awkward albatross dragging its wings on the ship's deck, is the object of men's mockery and cruelty. Even his mother curses God for having made her give birth to a poet; and his wife, after gleefully plotting to make him love her more than he loves God, moves from these "impious farces" to the exciting dream of tearing out the poet's heart and throwing it, with disdain, to her favorite animal. The poet accepts his suffering and humiliation as "a divine remedy for our impurities." Raising his arms toward Heaven, blind to the ferocity of his fellow men, the poet dreams of the "mystic crown" made of "pure light" which God will one day place on his noble head.

In the early poems of *Les Fleurs du mal,* the artist's alienation is expressed either as a total removal from human history or as a transcendent, nonhistorical relation to humanity. Both these alternatives consist in the resolving of uncertainty, conflict, and contradiction through a kind of vertical leap of consciousness. They are solutions to a problem which deserve to be treated as symptoms of the same problem, since they essentially involve the suppression of the problem and its disguised repetition. Thus, in "Les Phares" the power of art seems to be to deny the reality of suffering and to present it to God as "le meilleur témoignage / Que nous puissions donner de notre dignité." The curses, blasphemies, ecstasies, and tears which Baudelaire finds in the works of all the painters he has evoked in the first eight stanzas of the poem become a "divine opium" for the very mortals whose curses and complaints artists such as Goya and Delacroix have depicted. Represented in art, conflict and chaos magically become that which saves and directs an otherwise lost humanity:

> C'est un cri répété par mille sentinelles,
> Un ordre renvoyé par mille porte-voix;
> C'est un phare allumé sur mille citadelles,
> Un appel de chasseurs perdus dans les grands bois![1]

1. Theirs is a cry repeated by a thousand sentinels, an order passed on by a thousand messengers, a beacon lit upon a thousand citadels, the call of the huntsmen lost in the wide woods

Prose translations of Baudelaire's verse are from Francis Scarfe's *Baudelaire.* See note 1, Introduction.

"Les Phares" is faithful to a fundamental myth of Western culture: art sublimates suffering, and it can even rid us of suffering by adding something sublime to the expression of it. In Baudelaire's poem, the artistic representations of suffering become the guiding lights—"les phares"—for our exit from suffering. Nothing really has happened to human experience except that it has been moved upward; the "ardent sanglot qui roule d'âge en âge" dies out at the edge of God's eternity. "Les Phares" appears to announce that suffering ennobles; what it announces more obliquely is that the ennobling of suffering eliminates it.

The notions of the Ideal and of Ideal Beauty are intimately connected in Baudelaire with both knowledge and sexuality. The emergence of an erotic esthetic will also involve the eroticizing of knowledge. But in early poems such as "Elévation" and "La Beauté," the sexual imagery is merely juxtaposed with the epistemological claims. In "Elévation," the description of the poet's spirit plunging beyond the confines of the "starry spheres" suggests a sexual penetration ("Tu sillonnes gaiement l'immensité profonde / Avec une indicible et mâle volupté"), but this erotic "rising up" seems to have no effect on the nature of the poet's comprehension of "the language of flowers and of silent things." An effortless, serene understanding is unaffected by the erotic energy of the leap into understanding. In the same way, poets are presented as sensual lovers of beauty in "La Beauté": they are bruised at her breast, and her eyes fascinate these "do-

cile lovers." But Beauty herself is nonerotic and insensitive (she never cries or laughs, and she hates any
movement which "displaces lines"), and her majestic
attitudes, borrowed from "the proudest monu-
ments," plunge the poet into "austere studies." This
"dream of stone" ("Je suis belle, ô mortels! comme
un rêve de pierre") evokes the poet-lover's desiring
energies in order to arrest them, to transform them
into a contemplative fascination more fitting to the
intellectual puzzle of a mysterious, impenetrable
sphynx.

But even in the early section of *Les Fleurs du mal,*
the poet is talked about in other ways. We see the beginnings of a definition of poetic fantasy which
would remove it entirely from the axis of vertical
transcendence. In "Au Lecteur," the poem which in-
troduces *Les Fleurs du mal,* Baudelaire makes in the
first eight stanzas a lurid inventory of "the infamous
menagerie" of human vices. The effect of this inventory is somewhat ambiguous, for the panorama of
human vice is so extreme, so provokingly unqual-
ified, that we may find something unserious in it. The
poem is perhaps mainly a demonstration of the poet's
mastery of a certain insolence. He makes an eloquent,
high-handed, ingenious enumeration of obvious and
slightly less obvious sins, and we respond less to the
indictment than to the virtuosity of tone and the variety of diction in the poem. A repellently realistic description of vice alternates with the allegorization of
evil; and the poem moves between the eloquence of a
sermon and the casual, even snickering, tone of con-
nivance in evil.

The hidden strategy of the poem becomes apparent in the last two stanzas, in Baudelaire's famous description of *Ennui,* our worst vice:

> Il en est un plus laid, plus méchant, plus immonde!
> Quoiqu'il ne pousse ni grands gestes ni grands cris,
> Il ferait volontiers de la terre un débris
> Et dans un bâillement avalerait le monde;
>
> C'est l'Ennui!—l'oeil chargé d'un pleur involontaire,
> Il rêve d'échafauds en fumant son houka.
> Tu le connais, lecteur, ce monstre délicat,
> —Hypocrite lecteur,—mon semblable,—mon frère![2]

Boredom is not an evil in the same sense as, for example, self-satisfied remorse or stupidity or hypocrisy. Unlike these other evils mentioned in the poem, *Ennui* is a state in which *any* evil might be committed. Its peculiarity is to be empty; it is precisely because there is nothing in boredom itself that it accommodates anything. Other crimes are more dramatic; boredom neither makes great gestures nor utters loud cries. It is a vacuum; it would destroy the world merely by sucking it into its own void. But this is not too dissimilar from what Baudelaire describes as the esthetic state, as the artist's uncontrolled and unreserved openness to other forms of being.

2. there is one even uglier and more wicked and filthier than all the rest! Although it makes no frenzied gestures and utters no savage cries, yet it would fain reduce the earth to ruin, it would gladly swallow the world in one gaping yawn:

it is Boredom, *Tedium vitae,* who with an unwilling tear in his eye dreams of gibbets as he smokes his pipe. You know him, Reader, you know that fastidious monster—O hypocritical Reader, my fellow-man and brother!

"Au Lecteur" should alert us to a crucial aspect of
Les Fleurs du mal: Baudelaire is less concerned with a
serious classification of all the psychological and be-
havioral "flowers" which constitute "evil" than with
an imaginative promiscuity that leaves humanity indifferent to the ethical quality of the wildly heterogeneous scenes to which it "sacrifices" itself. We
will have occasion to see that crime in Baudelaire
is in fact a defensive strategy against the dangers of
that promiscuity. "Au Lecteur" already gives us a
hint of Baudelaire's fascination with the sheer mobility of fantasy, although the moralistic bias of the
poem restricts fantasy's field to a more or less conventional, predefined area of human vices. The poet's
condemnation of *Ennui* as the worst vice of all does,
however, suggest that the greatest threat in *Ennui* is
not the scenes which it may actually produce but
rather its very aptitude for producing scenes. The importance of this distinction will become apparent in
Les Fleurs du mal as soon as Baudelaire treats the
productivity of fantasy more directly and drops his
pose as judge of certain essentially allegorized deriva-
tions of fantasy. It is already clear that *Ennui* pro-
motes strictly imaginary violence: "Il rêve d'échafauds
en fumant son houka." *Ennui* is a "delicate monster,"
an armchair virtuoso of crime. In a sense, the whole
poem suggests Baudelaire's interest in something
light or insubstantial in vice. The poetic enumeration
of "the infamous menagerie of our vices" has been an
exercise in eloquence and elegance. The most somber
indictment of humanity has allowed Baudelaire to
demonstrate tonal variety and indeterminacy, and

thus in his opening poem, he is already subordinating a moralistic concern with "evil" (a concern parodistically illustrated by the taunting apostrophe to the reader) to a fascination with the creative mobility of fantasy.

Any such relocation, however, requires a willingness to be frank about the operations of fantasy, and Baudelaire's taunting reference to the reader suggests a universal conspiracy to deny the violence of imagination. The reader is a brother in fantasy-crimes, but he also is expected to reject hypocritically this complicity. This is exactly what Baudelaire does in the early poems of *Les Fleurs du mal*. "Au Lecteur" has both illustrated and explicitly stated the morally ambiguous nature of imagination, but it is immediately followed by a hypocritical denial of its own lesson. The poet becomes the noble, misunderstood, idealistic dreamer of "Bénédiction" and "Elévation"; and the guilty, devious brothers of the first poem are transformed, in "Les Phares," into a community of virtuous sentinels guiding one another through the tragic course of life and offering to God their very misery as testimony to their worth.

"Au Lecteur" creates certain reservations about the poetic idealism of the early poems of *Les Fleurs du mal* even before that idealism is proposed. Vertical transcendence is called into question in other ways. First of all, there is uncertainty about *where* the ideal is. The most clichéd answer to this places the ideal in a Christian eternity. But Baudelaire is also tempted to locate the alternative to a present reality of misery and cruelty in the past, especially in the poet's own past. However, the most personal memories are of a past which never took place. This is the nonhistorical past of "La Vie antérieure," which brings the possibility of an escape into the somber tableaux of death and time evoked in the three preceding poems ("Le Mauvais moine," "L'Ennemi," and "Le Guignon"). The deliberate unreality of the languid, voluptuous, luxurious past described in "La Vie antérieure" provides the first suggestion in *Les Fleurs du mal* of the atemporal nature of Baudelairean memory. Nostalgia for an infinitely desirable past brings the ideal down from a luminous and serene Heaven and makes it immanent to human history; an indifference to real historical time takes us one step further and implicitly redefines the ideal as the effect of certain mental processes. The historical reality of memories becomes inessential; both the real past and the imaginary past are evoked as the result of an abstraction from the experience of our senses. The mechanisms of this process will become clear when we examine "La Chevelure." The fabulous images of "La Vie antérieure" at least put us on the track of something crucial: the ideality of those "other" regions referred to by the poet (in pieces as different as "Bénédiction" and "La Vie antérieure") is not a function of their transcendent nature but rather of their status as mental fictions. It is by a certain kind of moving away from perceived realities that the poet succeeds in elaborating an absence which he makes historically intelligible by calling it a memory.

The senses are luxuriantly catered to in the setting of "La Vie antérieure" by the powerful harmonies of the waves, rich music, the scents of the naked slaves, and the cool touch of the palm leaves on the poet's forehead. But sensuality in the poem is continuously being qualified by certain intellectual operations. The vast porticoes are compared to basalt grottoes; in the second stanza the poet emphasizes reflections rather than direct perceptions (images from the sky are perceived in the sea's waves, and the waves' music blends with the colors of a sunset reflected by the poet's eyes); the "remembered" sensual feast is made somewhat insubstantial by the vague, general words used to describe it ("voluptés calmes," "splendeurs"). At the end of the poem the reader's attention is, like that of the slaves, drawn away from all the "voluptés" of this past life to the poet's "painful secret." The nature of that secret, which made the poet "languish," is irrelevant. It operates most effectively in the poem by almost erasing the poem's tableaux; the rich harmonies of sounds, colors, and odors give way to a fascination with an undefined (and therefore, for us, blank) interiority.

Nonetheless, it is important to emphasize the sensual richness of Baudelaire's "memories." The idealized past which he invents is usually one in which the senses are stimulated both by natural pleasures and by a profusion of man-made ornaments and furnishings. Poetic idealization thus begins to look like the very opposite of spiritualization; it is an abstracting process of the mind which returns the poet to sensual intensities. Finally, however, we should not try to stop Baudelairean movement either on the side of the senses or on the side of abstraction. The overpowering sensation, merely by virtue of its strength, propels us out of sensation; it spiritualizes itself by its very intensity.

This appears to be one of the more neglected meanings of "Correspondances." Readers of this poem have frequently been misled by the reference to Nature as containing "forests of symbols" in the first stanza. This presumably refers to a system of vertical correspondences: the "temple" of Nature is replete with symbols of spiritual reality. In fact, the metaphysical suggestiveness of the first four verses is simply dropped in the second and third stanzas. We move from vertical transcendence to horizontal "unity." "Les parfums, les couleurs et les sons se répondent": that is, stimuli ordinarily associated with one of our senses can produce sensations "belonging" to another sense. Baudelaire asserts, and in the third stanza illustrates, the reality of these analogies (certain perfumes, for example, are "green as fields"). "Correspondances" does present itself as a doctrinaire poem (thus the countless critical efforts to extract the doctrine, to find its sources in nineteenth-century esthetics, philosophy, and psychology), and the doctrine which the poem espouses and vaguely outlines has much less to do with symbolism in Nature than with a metaphorical unity within Nature. Comparisons using the word *comme* occur six times in the two middle stanzas, and we might think of this as a stylistic demonstration of those "echoes" of a distant likeness which the poet asks us to hear in each of our experiences.

But the last four verses of "Correspondances" bring us back to the metaphysically suggestive aspect of the

first stanza. This is done, however, not by a renewed
reference to symbols in Nature, but rather by an
abrupt shift in the metaphorical register. With certain
perfumes, the second term of the comparison can no
longer be designated; the specificity at the beginning of
the sonnet's first tercet gives way to the grand vague-
ness of the poem's concluding movement:

> Il est des parfums frais comme des chairs d'enfants,
> Doux comme les hautbois, verts comme les prairies,
> —Et d'autres, corrompus, riches et triomphants,
>
> Ayant l'expansion des choses infinies,
> Comme l'ambre, le musc, le bejoin et l'encens,
> Qui chantent les transports de l'esprit et des sens.[3]

What we can substitute for these "other" perfumes is
"infinite things." The expression is remarkably (and
effectively) imprecise. The poet is no longer compar-
ing one sensory experience to another; rather, certain
stimulants can, so to speak, carry the senses away
from themselves. They don't exactly remind us of
anything else; rather, they "expand" and they "trans-
port," they become "infinite things" (beyond the
senses) in their effects *on* the senses.

Sensuality spiritualizes: the final lines of "Correspondances" already point to this odd conclusion. It is
as if a maximal sensual intensity passed over into the

3. There are perfumes fresh and cool as the bodies of children,
mellow as oboes, green as fields; and others that are perverse, rich,
and triumphant,
   that have the infinite expansion of infinite things—such as
amber, musk, benjamin, and incense, which chant the ecstasies of
the mind and senses.

opposite of sensuality. Somehow that maximal point begins to create space; there is an "expansion" like that of "infinite things," and perhaps a certain emptiness insinuates itself into the plenitude of the senses. Baudelaire frequently expresses his intuition of this process as a fascination with disproportionately large forms or with the process of enlargement. In "Le Poème du haschisch," he insists that the "immense dream" produced by the drug is a "natural dream"; in hashish, we find "nothing miraculous at all, but rather our own nature exaggerated and magnified [le naturel excessif]" (354–55). Time and space undergo a "monstrous growth": the consumer of hashish "looks through the profound years with a certain melancholy pleasure and daringly plunges into infinite perspectives." In this "abnormal and tyrannical growth [accroissement]" of time and space, of feelings and ideas, lies the joy of being intoxicated with hashish (377). Also, Baudelaire finds it easy to tolerate and even enjoy Nature, provided it is—paradoxically—dematerialized by being "unnaturally" exaggerated or enlarged. One of Baudelaire's most relaxed evocations of a natural landscape is in the poem "La Géante," where the poet imagines living next to a young female giant "Du temps que la Nature en sa verve puissante / Concevait chaque jour des enfants monstrueux." He would have liked to sleep "nonchalantly" in the shadow of her breasts, like a peaceful hamlet at the foot of a mountain. The young giant is a pleasantly grotesque image of Nature expanded, and the poet's relation to her exemplifies a sensuality pacified and partially spiritualized by the exaggeration of natural forms.

4
Cradling

The movement in sensation away from sensation is central to Baudelaire's love poetry. In "La Chevelure," "L'Invitation au voyage," "Le Beau navire," "Le Balcon," and "Les Bijoux," we find Baudelaire's most complete and most original expression of a psychology of mobile desiring fantasy. Consider the ambiguous sexuality of "La Chevelure":

> O toison, moutonnant jusque sur l'encolure!
> O boucles! O parfum chargé de nonchaloir!
> Extase! Pour peupler ce soir l'alcôve obscure
> Des souvenirs dormant dans cette chevelure,
> Je la veux agiter dans l'air comme un mouchoir!
>
> La langoureuse Asie et la brûlante Afrique,
> Tout un monde lointain, absent, presque défunt,
> Vit dans tes profondeurs, forêt aromatique!
> Comme d'autres esprits voguent sur la musique,
> Le mien, ô mon amour! nage sur ton parfum.
>
> J'irai là-bas où l'arbre et l'homme, pleins de sève,
> Se pâment longuement sous l'ardeur des climats;
> Fortes tresses, soyez la houle qui m'enlève!
> Tu contiens, mer d'ébène, un éblouissant rêve
> De voiles, de rameurs, de flammes et de mâts:
>
> Un port retentissant où mon âme peut boire
> A grands flots le parfum, le son et la couleur;

Où les vaisseaux, glissant dans l'or et dans la moire,
Ouvrent leurs vastes bras pour embrasser la gloire
D'un ciel pur où frémit l'éternelle chaleur.

Je plongerai ma tête amoureuse d'ivresse
Dans ce noir océan où l'autre est enfermé;
Et mon esprit subtil que le roulis caresse
Saura vous retrouver, ô féconde paresse!
Infinis bercements du loisir embaumé!

Cheveux bleus, pavillon de ténèbres tendues,
Vous me rendez l'azur du ciel immense et rond;
Sur les bords duvetés de vos mèches tordues
Je m'enivre ardemment des senteurs confondues
De l'huile de coco, du musc et du goudron.

Longtemps! toujours! ma main dans ta crinière lourde
Sèmera le rubis, la perle et le saphir,
Afin qu'à mon désir tu ne sois jamais sourde!
N'es-tu pas l'oasis où je rêve, et la gourde
Où je hume à longs traits le vin du souvenir?[1]

1.   *Hair*
O fleece, billowing down to the neck, O locks, O fragrance laden
with languidness! O ecstasy! This night, to people the dark alcove
of our love with all the memories that slumber in your hair, I long
to wave it in the air as one waves a handkerchief.

All languid Asia, blazing Africa, a whole faraway world that is
absent, almost dead, survives in the depths of this forest of aromas;
and as other spirits [sail on] music, so mine, O my beloved, [floats]
upon your perfume.

I shall go there where men and trees, full of the sap of life, swoon
in the ardent heats; dense tresses, be the swell that carries me away,
for you contain, O sea of ebony, a dazzling dream of sails and
oarsmen, flames, and masts;

an echoing port where my soul may drink long waves of perfume, sound, and colour; in which the ships that glide in gold and
multicoloured silk, open wide their arms to embrace the splendour
of an immaculate sky that shimmers with everlasting heat;

Making love is obliquely referred to several times in "La Chevelure": in the images of trees and men full of sap, of boats gliding in gold and watered silk and opening their "arms" to embrace the sky, of a head plunging into a black ocean, and, more generally, in all the references to undulating rhythms suggestive of the movements in sex of lovers' bodies. But if we see mainly this, we see just enough to admire a certain kind of cleverness: through his description of the sea and the exotic country he invokes, Baudelaire manages to communicate considerable sexual detail without ever seeming to mention sex. But there is much more to the poem than a strategic elusiveness. Or rather, it is this very elusiveness about sex which justifies our thinking of "La Chevelure" as a poem about sexual intensities.

The subject of "La Chevelure" is desire. In *The Interpretation of Dreams* (1900), Freud speaks of *Wunsch* (translated as "wish" in the Standard Edition) as a psychic movement [eine psychische Regung] which aims to revive perceptual memories associated with

---

I shall plunge my head, [in love with drunkenness], into the jet-black ocean that contains the other sea; and my subtle mind, caressed by the rolling swell, will know how to find you there, O fertile indolence, infinite [rocking] of sweet-scented leisure!

Blue hair, tent hung with shadows, you bring me the azure of the great round sky, and on the downy shores of your plaited locks I grow drunk with the mingled scents of coconut-oil, and musk, and tar.

O long, O forever, my hand in your ponderous mane will sow rubies and pearls and sapphires, so that you will ever hearken to my desire: for you are the oasis of my dreaming, the gourd from which I drink long draughts of the wine of memory.

the satisfaction of a need.[2] The movement of desire is a movement of fantasy; it is an activity which produces images. In a sense, desire is always a lack. The object is never entirely present in desire; when it is, it erases desire. But at the same time, desire is never only a lack: certain fantasies (mental movements) both provide the necessary stimulus to desire and partially satisfy it. A fantasy-satisfaction anticipates the "real" satisfaction. Before physically going toward the object of desire, we psychically go toward it and, to a certain extent, already find pleasure in it.

But going toward the object in fantasy may be equivalent to going away from it. A psychologically reductive reading of Baudelaire's love poetry might speak of the poet's inability to establish any "exchange" with the desired woman, of his retreat from "direct" sexuality into a private world of fantasy. In a sense Baudelaire does ignore the woman; what I'm proposing is that his turning away from her is the sign of his intense desire for her. "La Chevelure" is a luxuriant demonstration of sexuality as inseparable from fantasy. This means that the desire to experience even the sharpest sensation has something abstract about it. The fantasies within which desire moves are purely mental, nonconcrete ways of appropriating sensation. In "La Chevelure," desire for the loved one is satisfied as the poet moves within the intervals separating her image from the other images she gives

2. *The Interpretation of Dreams,* in *The Standard Edition of the Complete Psychological Works of Sigmund Freud,* ed. James Strachey (London: Hogarth Press, 1953–66), 5:565–66. References to *The Standard Edition* will henceforth be abbreviated as *SE.*

rise to in the poet's fantasies. Precisely because she is the object of desire, she initiates desires which remove the poet from her; the woman exists for Baudelaire, not in order to satisfy his desires, but in order to produce them.

Where do the fantasies of desire originate? The references to memory in "La Chevelure" ("souvenir[s]" occurs in the first stanza and it is the final word of the poem) suggest that the poem's images belong to the poet's past. The notion of desire as an attempt to resurrect a lost pleasure is crucial to Freud's ideas about object-finding in sex. In part, what seems like a rather pedestrian if unobjectionable theory of desire in Freud (we seek to revive past satisfactions) serves the imprisonment of human sexuality within familial patterns of desire. For our earliest erotic satisfactions are at the mother's breast, and it is after speaking of suckling at the mother's breast as the "prototype of every relation of love" that Freud makes his celebrated remark, in *Three Essays on the Theory of Sexuality* (1905) that "the finding of an object is in fact a refinding of it."[3]

Baudelaire's poetry both confirms and subverts this mnemonic concept of desire. In "La Chevelure," the fact that the woman is nowhere in the fantasies inspired by her body suggests that, in a sense, she was never the real source of pleasure. I don't mean this in an anecdotal sense: there is no hidden meaning in the poem suggesting that this woman was never really satisfying in the first place. Rather, the poet's extravagant departure from the body he is lying close to

3. *SE*, 7:222.

could indicate that the past satisfactions revived in desire are themselves desiring fantasies. If we were to generalize the lesson of "La Chevelure," we would say: the objects of our sexual desires are fantasy-objects. If sexual desire is inseparable from fantasy, then it is always already an interpretative movement, and any originally exciting object or event gets lost in the very excitement which it produces. The work of fantasy in desire makes impossible the historical tracing of presumed sources of desire.

Freud himself makes a crucial step toward this position when, in his analysis of the "Wolf Man" case, he leaves room for some doubt about whether or not his patient actually observed, at the age of one-and-a-half, a scene of anal intercourse between his parents. That scene may be a fantasy-construct, a retroactive interpretation, Freud suggests, of sex between animals. This interpretation is made possible by the "Wolf Man's" own sexual development by the age of four (when he had the dream the analysis of which points to the scene of parental intercourse). Freud's discussion of this case strikingly illustrates his hesitation between a realistic view of the "primal scene" and an understanding of it as one of the fantasy-scenarios by which the child may both solve certain enigmas (such as birth or the difference between the sexes) and adjust the past to his present sexual needs and capacities. (It's true that the realistic view is exceptionally resilient. If the "primal scene" didn't actually take place in the individual's past, it took place in the past of the race and our memory of it would then be part of our racial inheritance.

This phylogenetic thesis is already proposed in the "Wolf Man" case.)[4]

Jean Laplanche, taking the very passage from the *Three Essays* which I mentioned a moment ago and which would seem to support a theory of sexual desire as an attempt to repeat the sexually satisfying possession of the real mother's real breast in infancy, even argues that the breast becomes an object of sexual desire (rather than merely a source of nourishment) only as an internalized fantasy-object. Sexual excitement would be *identical to* a psychic movement which submits reality to the passionate interpretations of desire.[5] This is dramatically illustrated in Baudelaire's "La Chevelure" by the total absence of the woman from the fantasies evoked by her presence. If the pleasure which she has given the poet has always been inseparable from the operations of his desiring fantasies, the woman is best remembered when she is continuously being forgotten.

The objects of desire are not objects; they are crea-

4. It is the essay "From the History of an Infantile Neurosis" (1918; in *SE,* 8) which is commonly known as the "Wolf Man" case. The case was first written up in 1914. It is in his 1918 additions to the earlier version that Freud is most sympathetic to the thesis of retroactive fantasies. However, even in the first version he emphasizes the fact that the child's understanding and interpretation of the "primal scene" is "deferred" until the age of four.

5. See *Vie et mort en psychanalyse* (Paris: Flammarion, 1970), pp. 30–37. Laplanche's extraordinary (and highly readable) work is indispensable for an understanding of recent psychoanalytic thought in France. An excellent translation by Jeffrey Mehlman is now available: *Life and Death in Psychoanalysis* (Baltimore: Johns Hopkins University Press, 1976).

tive processes. In a sense, this liberates memory from time. More precisely, desiring fantasies are by no means turned only toward the past; they are projective reminiscences. This is suggested in "La Chevelure" by the fact that the references to memory enclose several stanzas in which the dominant tense is, either explicitly or implicitly, the future. The *souvenirs* of the fourth verse seem to announce a past; instead, a certain future is energetically willed until it becomes the present (in stanza six), and finally, in the last stanza, the poet promises to renew, in the future, this summoning up of an intoxicating past, this process of remembering which consists of the most willfully pursued projects.[6]

The movements in "La Chevelure" between sensation and fantasy, and between the present and the future (a future equated with the past), duplicate a physical movement which is at the heart of the poem: the movement of rocking or of cradling. *Bercement* is, to use a Proustian expression, one of the "fundamental notes" of Baudelaire's imagination. Perhaps the purest pleasure Baudelaire can imagine is to be rocked as boats are rocked on a gentle sea. When, in "Le Peintre de la vie moderne," he speaks of the "immense jouissance" of passionately observing crowds of people in a big city, the pleasure he describes is that of "making one's home in multiplicity, in swaying movement, in everything fugitive and in the infinite [élire domicile

6. For an extremely subtle discussion of "the dialectics of intoxication" in "La Chevelure," and of the inebriating nature of will itself for Baudelaire, see Victor Brombert, "The Will to Ecstasy: The Example of Baudelaire's 'La Chevelure'," in *Yale French Studies,* no. 50 (1974).

dans le nombre, dans l'ondoyant, dans le mouvement, dans le fugitif et l'infini]" (1160). Also, Baudelaire's interest in women is frequently expressed as a fascination with their swaying movements as they walk. The "boat" in the poem "Le Beau navire" is a woman, and her clothes are like the sails of a ship moving into the open sea "Suivant un rhythme doux, et paresseux, et lent." What is it about the sea, and especially about a boat's swaying movements, which leads Baudelaire to associate "robust ships, with their idle and homesick air," with a promise of happiness, and even to speak of the spectacle of the sea as providing "the highest idea of beauty offered to man in his transient abode"? (*Journaux intimes,* 1253, 1290).

Most obviously, Baudelaire's association of happiness with a boat being "cradled" by the sea points to a particularly strong if sublimated memory of the bliss of being cradled in infancy. The emphasis on the sea even suggests the memory of a prenatal life in the liquid environment of the womb, of being carried along on an inner sea by the boat-mother's movements. But "La Chevelure" should help us to see the inadequacy of speculations about the "original" appeal of *bercement;* the body's pleasure in being cradled can be primarily an occasion for expanding the very notion of cradling. The fifth stanza of the poem is a climax. The verses are exclamatory; the tone is insistently willful; and it is as if this concentrated energy propelled the poet into the physical reality of his fantasies and therefore allowed for the present tense of stanza six, the "arrival" or actual realization of the dream. The climax of stanza five could also be thought of as a

sexual climax: a powerful, culminating sexual experience is suggested by the image of the "tête amoureuse
d'ivresse" plunging into the dark ocean, as well as by
the association of fecundity with the state of idleness
finally achieved. But at the same time that is the most
abstract stanza of the entire poem. The word *bercements,* by its strategic placement in the stanza and in the
poem, is revealed as the principal "memory" with
which the poet has been seeking to fill the dark alcove.
But the physical meaning of *bercements* is practically
canceled out by the abstractions surrounding the word:
"féconde paresse," "infinis," "loisir embaumé." It is
as if the very desire to be gently rocked gave birth to
the desire for a kind of abstract cradling.

In "Fusées" (one of the sections of the *Journaux intimes*), Baudelaire writes that ". . . the infinite and
mysterious charm which lies in the contemplation of a
ship, especially of a ship in motion," depends in part on
"the successive multiplication and the generating of all
the curves and imaginary figures executed in space by
the real elements of the object" (1261). To watch a
moving ship is to observe the *passage* from the "real"
to the "imaginary," the actual "generating" of multiple, nonconcrete, constantly disappearing shapes by a
material object. In the same way, the references in "La
Chevelure" to bodies being gently rocked (in sex and
on the sea) appear to "generate" an imaginary version
of *bercement.* The swaying of a drunkenly amorous
"head" in the woman's "sea" is also the "caressing" of
an "esprit subtil." And this (phallic) mind enjoys being
cradled by a state of being, by the infinite rocking motions of scented leisure. The meaning of *bercement* itself

is therefore rocked between the physical and the mental. But, as I have suggested, the entire poem is about a similar kind of rocking or cradling. In the mental movements of his desire, the poet finds an abstract version of the regularly swaying motion to which his body seeks to return. The memory of the bliss of being cradled appears to have sensitized him to the pleasure of the cradling movement in the very desire to be cradled—and, by implication, in all desire.

Sexual desire, "La Chevelure" suggests, is an appetite for sensations which generates the imaginary. Thus the "infinite and mysterious charm" of a boat moving on the sea may be its analogy with the "charm" of desiring. "La Chevelure" gives a special twist to the Freudian concept of *Nachträglichkeit*. The deferred interpretation of a childhood experience is not made only as a result of a sexual development which retroactively makes the past sexually meaningful (or even reworks it to create a sexual scenario). Cradling is partly sexualized as a result of the connection established between the lovers' bodies and gently rocking movements, but *bercement* is also reinterpreted in order to cover the pleasure of an ontological discovery. Scenes of cradling movement (a boat on the sea, the poet being carried on the woman's hair, an infant being rocked in a cradle) are perhaps all equally pleasurable representations of the pleasurable movements of sexual desire.

5
Teasing

If "La Chevelure" raises the question of where the woman is in the poet's desire for her, Baudelaire's love poetry also raises the question of where the poet is in his desire. The mobility of the desiring imagination makes the identity of the desiring self problematic. The movement away from the woman's physical presence is also a movement away from any fixed center of being in the poet. Sexuality sets into motion a kind of fantasy-machine. But it is not only the woman as an identifiable, stable object of desire who gets lost in the turning of that machine; the poet himself is set afloat among his fantasies, and the more intensely he desires the less possible it becomes to say anything conclusive about his desires.

The metamorphoses of the woman within the poet's fantasies create impressive margins of freedom for Baudelaire, margins which allow him not only to avoid being fixed on any impoverishing center within himself, but also to escape any obsessive attachment to the loved one. All the images in "Le Serpent qui danse," for example, express a playful indefiniteness in the poet's feelings about the woman; he tries them out through a variety of comparisons which shift the woman around in somewhat the same way as a "jongleur sacré" rocks a snake back and forth at the end of a stick. There are, it's true, suggestions of the woman's coldness: her eyes are "deux bijoux froids où se mêle / L'or avec le fer," and her saliva, which the poet drinks, is compared to "un flot grossi par la fonte / Des glaciers grondants." But the "portrait" of the woman is much less coherent in "Le Serpent qui danse" than in the poem immediately preceding it, *Avec ses vêtements ondoyants et nacrés,* in which the image of a serpent on a stick is merely an ornamental aspect in the delineation of a fixed character (that of the cold, sterile woman). In "Le Serpent qui danse," psychology is dissipated by all the substitutions for the woman in the poet's vision. First of all, as in "La Chevelure," the poet's "âme rêveuse"—"Comme un navire qui s'éveille / Au vent du matin"—gets ready to depart for a distant land on the "mer odorante et vagabonde" of the woman's perfumed hair. And that "departure" is accomplished through a series of slightly insolent, dehumanizing images: the woman's shimmering skin is like "une étoffe vacillante," her laziness makes her childlike head sway "avec la mollesse / D'un jeune éléphant," and her body, as she bends over and lies down, is compared to "un fin vaisseau / Qui roule bord sur bord et plonge / Ses vergues dans l'eau." Finally, the most crudely sensual image of the poem—that of the poet licking the saliva from the woman's teeth—is metamorphosed into impersonal, grandiose visions of Nature: the melting glaciers and the "liquid sky" which, at the end of the poem, sprinkles the poet's heart with stars as he drinks the intoxicating saliva. Snake, elephant, and boat: the "real" woman is dismissed by and into these images, and at the same time it becomes impossible to locate the poet's desire for her. Readers of "Le Serpent qui danse" have generally emphasized what Jean Prévost calls "the warding off of desire" by bizarre and slightly comical images.[1] But it could also be said that Baudelaire gives us desire uninhibited by psychological fascination. The woman's physical presence is actually rendered in considerable detail in "Le Serpent qui danse," while at the same time almost every stanza of the poem illustrates the "generating" of imaginary forms as a result of the volatilizing pressure of desire on "the real elements of the object." The intense play of desire does away with the woman's body as a precise cause of precise desires. "Le Serpent qui danse" is an exercise in pure metaphor.

There is a happy psychic mobility in Baudelaire. The cradling rhythms of desire and the metamorphoses which accompany them are, in poems such as "La Chevelure," "Le Serpent qui danse," "Le Parfum" and "Le Cadre" (poems II and III of "Un Fantôme"), and "L'Invitation au voyage," sources of a luxuriant serenity. The latter poem is perhaps Baudelaire's most extraordinary achievement in the rendering of a richly indeterminate eroticism. The poet's "invitation" is actually an accumulation of withdrawn suggestions. The very first appeal to the woman's desire is already an unanchoring of desire:

1. Prévost even speaks of a "remedy for sexuality" in these images. See his *Baudelaire / Essai sur l'inspiration et la création poétiques* (Paris: Mercure de France, 1953), pp. 251–52.

> Mon enfant, ma soeur,
> Songe à la douceur
> D'aller là-bas vivre ensemble![2]

Who is being invited? Is the woman child, sister, or mistress? And where would she and the poet go? The vague "là-bas," it later turns out, is a country which resembles the woman, who, by the end of the first stanza, has become a mysteriously sorrowful mistress with treacherous eyes. The correspondences between the country and the woman or the poet would seem to suggest an inner landscape:

> Tout y parlerait
> A l'âme en secret
> Sa douce langue natale.[3]

But the allegorization of the country is subverted by the care with which its materiality is evoked: most of the second stanza creates the setting of a room with shining old furniture, rare flowers and the smell of amber, richly decorated ceilings and "deep" mirrors. Finally, however, the visual elements of each stanza are pushed into the background by the incantatory abstractions of the refrain which follows all three stanzas: "Là, tout n'est qu'ordre et beauté, / Luxe, calme et volupté." The voyage *is* the swaying in-definiteness of the invitation: the hesitation about the nature of the relation between the poet and the

2. My child, my sister, imagine the happiness of voyaging there to spend our lives together
3. [Everything there would] whisper in secret to our souls in their own gentle mother-tongue.

woman, the mystery of her treacherous sorrow, the doubt about the place as an inner landscape or a real country, the movement between the intimate tone and concrete details of the stanzas and the austere abstractions of the refrain, and finally the alternation between verses of five syllables and verses of seven syllables (both uneven, both creating a rhythmical impression of incompleteness). The place of the loved one and of the country is unlocatable in the poet's invitation to her to accompany him there. The most sensual aspect of "L'Invitation au voyage" is perhaps its untroubled, somewhat perverse elusiveness; the poem is a tease, and with his teasing, shifting tone and his mobile attention the poet protects both his own and the woman's indeterminacy of being.

And yet there is the refrain of "L'Invitation au voyage" which provides, for all its own elusive abstractness, a kind of anchoring point of return for each of the poem's major movements. Desire dislocates attention, and Baudelaire appears to work most securely with the disruptive movements of desire when movement is contained and structured by recurrence. He is one of the most artful manipulators in the history of poetry of the phenomenon of return—from the return of individual sounds to that of an entire stanza.[4] The simultaneous operation of various levels

4. See the dazzling, exhaustive (and exhausting) analysis of "Les Chats" by Claude Lévi-Strauss and Roman Jakobson, "'Les Chats' de Baudelaire," *L'Homme* 2, no. 1 (1962). Michael Riffaterre has written a persuasive critique of this reading: "Describing Poetic Structures: Two Approaches to Baudelaire's 'Les Chats'," in *Structuralism,* ed. Jacques Ehrmann (New York: Anchor Books, 1970). This volume originally appeared as an issue of *Yale French Studies* in

of recurrence—phonemic, syntactic, semantic—is responsible for the complex musicality of, for example, "Le Balcon," "Harmonie du soir," "L'Irréparable," and "Moesta et errabunda." Nothing could be more alien to *Les Fleurs du mal* than Rimbaud's chimerical attempt, in the *Illuminations,* to eliminate repetition. In his most radical work, Rimbaud is testing the possibility of a poetic utterance devoid of all structural references, an entirely new utterance without depth and with no past. This is also Rimbaud's dream for the self, for that "other I" which would not be constrained by consistency, continuity, or depth. Baudelaire, on the other hand, embraces repetition with what we might call a sensual prudence. The centrifugal movement of desire—the movement of fantasy away from the object of desire—is controlled, at least formally, by compositional returns to points of departure. It is as if an intuition about desire as *always elsewhere* were partially negated by demonstrations of the poem returning to itself.

When that return is most elaborately plotted, Baudelairean memory itself may be reduced to the status of a historically accurate record. This is the case in the impressive poem "Le Balcon," in which the poet evokes a time in the future when his mistress will remember a happiness which seems now to be on the point of disappearing. The woman is once again a reservoir of memories (she is addressed as "Mère des souvenirs, maîtresse des maîtresses"), but memory

---

1966. Riffaterre's essay has been reprinted in his *Essais de stylistique structurale* (Paris: Flammarion, 1971).

in "Le Balcon," instead of removing the poet from his past, will merely return him to the moment of actual intimacy with the beloved: "Car à quoi bon chercher tes beautés langoureuses / Ailleurs qu'en ton cher corps et qu'en ton coeur si doux?" Everything in the poem invites us to experience the pleasures of returning: the evocation of the lovers' peaceful intimacy, the use of the same line as both the first and the last verses in each of the six five-line stanzas, the internal rhymes and the structural repetitions which create the incantatory rhythms of several lines in the poem (for example: "O toi, tous mes plaisirs! ô toi, tous mes devoirs!" [line 2], "Que ton sein m'était doux! que ton coeur m'était bon!" [line 8], and "Que l'espace est profond! que le coeur est puissant!" [line 12]). "Le Balcon" has a heavy, claustrophobic beauty. The somewhat melancholy happiness it describes is submitted to so many disciplinary enclosures that we may feel inclined to locate the subject of the poem not in its obliquely told love story, but rather in the poetic ingenuities which make our reading of the poem an experience as repetitive, or as circular, as the natural cycle, referred to in the last stanza, of the daily rising and setting of the sun. The curve of the arc along which fantasy moves is barely extended beyond the point of departure; the cradling movements of "Le Balcon" are almost indistinguishable from the monotonous *jouissance* of sameness.

6
Bits and Pieces

In "Le Balcon," we see the possibility of a certain closing in on the movements of desire. The extremes to which Baudelaire finally goes in an effort to immobilize fantasy will make more sense if we first look more closely at the unanchoring effects of desire on the poet's and the woman's identities. In much of "La Chevelure," the poet is not addressing the woman, but rather her hair. He is speaking directly to a part of her body, and as if this part could be detached: "Je la [la chevelure] veux agiter dans l'air comme un mouchoir!" The trivial image of a handkerchief being shaken in the air adds to the poet's erotic interest a note of comic insolence not unlike the comparison of the loved one to a young elephant or to a serpent at the end of a stick in "Le Serpent qui danse." Furthermore, the hair passes through various metamorphoses—from fleece to forest to ocean—under the pressure of the poet's attentive desire. Thus the poet is attracted by what almost appears to be a detachable part of the woman, a part which displays a striking aptitude for metamorphoses and displacements.

A more radical version of this takes place in "Le Beau navire" and in "Les Bijoux." Here is "Le Beau navire":

Je veux te raconter, ô molle enchanteresse!
Les diverses beautés qui parent ta jeunesse;
        Je veux te peindre ta beauté,
Où l'enfance s'allie à la maturité.

Quand tu vas balayant l'air de ta jupe large,
Tu fais l'effet d'un beau vaisseau qui prend le large,
        Chargé de toile, et va roulant
Suivant un rhythme doux, et paresseux, et lent.

Sur ton cou large et rond, sur tes épaules grasses,
Ta tête se pavane avec d'étranges grâces;
        D'un air placide et triomphant
Tu passes ton chemin, majestueuse enfant.

Je veux te raconter, ô molle enchanteresse!
Les diverses beautés qui parent ta jeunesse;
        Je veux te peindre ta beauté,
Où l'enfance s'allie à la maturité.

Ta gorge qui s'avance et qui pousse la moire,
Ta gorge triomphante est une belle armoire
        Dont les panneaux bombés et clairs
Comme les boucliers accrochent des éclairs;

Boucliers provoquants, armés de pointes roses!
Armoire à doux secrets, pleine de bonnes choses,
        De vins, de parfums, de liqueurs
Qui feraient délirer les cerveaux et les coeurs!

Quand tu vas balayant l'air de ta jupe large
Tu fais l'effet d'un beau vaisseau qui prend le large,
        Chargé de toile, et va roulant
Suivant un rhythme doux, et paresseux, et lent.

Tes nobles jambes, sous les volants qu'elles chassent,
Tourmentent les désirs obscurs et les agacent,
        Comme deux sorcières qui font
Tourner un philtre noir dans un vase profond.

Tes bras, qui se joueraient des précoces hercules,
Sont des boas luisants les solides émules,
　　Faits pour serrer obstinément,
Comme pour l'imprimer dans ton coeur, ton amant.

Sur ton cou large et rond, sur tes épaules grasses,
Ta tête se pavane avec d'étranges grâces;
　　D'un air placide et triomphant
Tu passes ton chemin, majestueuse enfant.[1]

The appeal of cradling rhythms has led Baudelaire to something more radical than the *bercements* of "La Chevelure." In "Le Beau navire," the poet's attention, in one sense, never wanders from the woman; it is while he is gazing fixedly at her in order to narrate or paint her beauties that a part of her body suddenly appears as an armoire and as a shield armed with pink tips. The process of fantasy-removal in stanzas five and six and again in stanzas eight and nine is significantly

---

1.　　　　　　　*The Beautiful Ship*
I want to describe to you, O tender enchantress, the various beauties which adorn your youth: I want to depict your loveliness in which childhood and maturity combine.

When you walk, sweeping the air with your ample skirt, you give the impression of a handsome ship setting out to sea with all its canvas spread, and swinging away, keeping a gentle, languid, slow rhythm.

On your broad, round throat, on your plump shoulders, your head sways with many a strange grace; with a placid, conquering air you go your way, majestic child.

I want to describe to you, O tender enchantress, the various beauties which adorn your youth; I want to depict your loveliness in which childhood and maturity combine.

Your jutting breast which curves the watered–silk, your triumphant breast is [a beautiful armoire], whose rounded, bright panels catch the light like shields: provoking shields, armed with rosy

different from what we found in "La Chevelure." The scent of the woman's hair in the latter poem transports the poet to other climates; it gives birth to scenes far removed from the lovers' dark alcove. And the erotic nature of the "original" scene continues to be present only in the description of scenes very different from it. When the poet reaches the country of his desiring imagination, it is almost as if, rather bizarrely, he had to remember where his body really is, and his memory of sex which is at once present and absent enters indirectly through references to his "subtle mind" being rocked by the waves' caress and to trees and men "full of sap." In "Le Beau navire," the woman's body is not left; it *becomes* that which is different from it. Instead of a process of willed but gently performed distancing from the woman, we have sudden, unexplained metamorphoses. The poet executes a fantasy-movement away from the woman which is not—as it

---

tips—[an armoire] full of delicious secrets, full of good things, with wines and perfumes and liqueurs that would fill men's minds and hearts with delirium.

When you walk, sweeping the air with your ample skirt, you give the impression of a handsome ship setting out to sea with all its canvas spread, and swinging away, keeping a gentle, languid, slow rhythm.

Your noble legs, under the flounces which they thrust before them, torment and tease obscure desires, like twin witches stirring a black potion in a deep vessel.

Your arms, which would be more than a match for an infant Hercules, are worthy rivals of glistening boas, fashioned for relentless embraces, as though to imprint your lover on your heart.

On your broad, round throat, on your plump shoulders, you head sways with many a strange grace; with a placid, conquering air you go your way, majestic child.

was in "La Chevelure"—an elaboration of other set-
tings based on easily recognizable properties of a real
object (from the undulating hair to the sea, from the
hair's scent to rare perfumes), but which is rather a leap
into an otherness equated with the same. The woman
excites the poet's metaphorical imagination into seeing
her as a succession of partial, discontinuous images.
The "story" of her beauty (which the poet announced
his intention to narrate in the first stanza) becomes a
floating of fragmented attributes and meanings.

It seems to me that such fragmentation can best be
understood in the light of some recent reformulations
of the psychoanalytic notion of a castration complex.[2]
For Freud, castration is first of all a solution to a problem, that of the anatomical difference between the
sexes. The basic assumption of sexual "theory" in
early childhood would be that a penis was given to
everyone. Those people who don't have one must
have had it taken away, and little girls presumably feel
the need to deny or make up for their lack of a penis.
The castration complex comes later, and it is crucially
linked with the Oedipus complex. The young boy
fears castration as a punishment, inflicted by his father,
for his sexual yearnings for his mother. In the case of

2. It's true that the "piece-by-piece" celebration of a woman's
beauty is not original with Baudelaire: it occurs, for example, in
litanies to the Blessed Virgin and in the "Blazons" of Renaissance
poetry. But there is no reason to assume that the tradition itself
would be invulnerable to interpretations similar to the one proposed here. Furthermore Baudelaire's interest in this poetic con-
vention is in itself something we may legitimately wish to account
for. Finding precedents for certain choices doesn't exhaust the
intelligibility of the choices.

the little girl, according to Freud, the castration complex precedes the Oedipal stage and allows her to enter
into the Oedipal triangle (by way of desiring the
father's penis). For the little boy, the terror of castration makes possible the end of the Oedipal stage, that
is, the renunciation of the mother, the entrance into the
latency period, and the introjection of the threatening
father as the superego or conscience.

But genital castration may be only one form of the
castration complex. Freud himself, in the 1917 essay
"On Transformations of Instinct as Exemplified in
Anal Eroticism," points out the analogy which the
child establishes in fantasy between the penis and other
detachable objects, especially feces and the child himself (who at birth detaches himself from his mother's
body). A chain of symbolic equations develops, the
real terms of which either do in fact detach themselves
from the person (for example, feces, gifts, and money),
or are seen as detachable in emotionally charged and
frequently violent fantasies of mutilation and incorpo-
ration (penis and breasts). There has been much debate
in the history of psychoanalysis about whether or not
this broadening of the notion of a castration complex
necessarily relocates its origins. Freud, for example,
while expressing his interest in the diverse manifesta-
tions of anguish over loss of or separation from a pre-
cious object, argued, in *Inhibitions, Symptoms and Anxiety,* (1926 [1925]), against Rank's view of castration
anxiety as a derivative of the birth trauma. For our
purposes, it will suffice simply to mention this debate
about origins and to point out that the hypothesis of a
first term in the symbolic "castration chain" is ex-

tremely problematic. And this by virtue of the fact that it is impossible in psychoanalysis to isolate any term from the fantasy operations which, by nature, ruin the clarities of history.

In their discussion of the symbolic value of the phallus, Jean Laplanche and J.-B. Pontalis reject both fixed allegorical meanings (the phallus as a sign of power or fertility) as well as the reduction of the phallus to the male sexual organ. Instead, they propose that we think of the phallus "as meaning [comme signification], as that which is symbolized in the most diverse representations."[3] This remark is extremely suggestive: it points to a formulation of the castration complex in terms of *an anguished preoccupation with the mobility of meaning.* Each of the terms in the symbolic equation mentioned a moment ago is something detached from a "mother-body," from a real or imagined totality, something which moves away and is transformed. There is no single reality "represented" in the movements of all these objects (child, feces, penis, breast, money); what they all have in common is the transforming movement away. In each case, a fantasy of wholeness seems to depend on the movement *not* taking place. The self's integrity is threatened by the infant's separation from its mother; the body's wholeness is destroyed by the actual or fantasized loss of feces or of the penis. The body no longer makes sense when something drops away from it.

3. *Vocabulaire de la psychanalyse* (Paris, 1973), p. 312. This exceptionally useful encyclopedia of psychoanalytic terms has been translated as *The Language of Psycho-analysis* by Donald Nicholson-Smith (New York, 1974).

On the other hand, the phallus becomes meaningful only by detaching itself from the body. It is not the phallic objects themselves which symbolize meaning. As long as the penis remains on the body, it has no general symbolic value; it is only in castration that, by threatening a constituted whole, it becomes the "figure" for a mysterious "ex-centricity" of the self—for the scattering of psychic coherence. Castration carries this symbolic value in two ways: each phallic object illustrates the phenomenon of a detachable, transformable part of a whole, and, more generally, the very quality of being detachable and movable is illustrated in the symbolic equations themselves, where moving significance is constantly moving among different representations of moving significance. If, as Freud suggests in his study of "little Hans,"[4] making the distinction between having and not having a penis is an important exercise in a binary structuring of reality, the detachable penis is only one term in a chain of phallic objects all of which create, by virtue of their mobility, epistemological disarray—a "castration complex" over fragmented sense.

What is it exactly which is felt to be set afloat in castration? The description of the phallus as a detachable, circulating object should remind us of Freud's description of desire. Desire is movement in the sense of being a mental activity designed to reactivate a scene connected in the past with the experience of pleasure. It immediately moves away from the desired object in order to develop a desiring fantasy which already in-

4. "Analysis of a Phobia in a Five-Year-Old Boy" (1909).

cludes a certain satisfaction. It is therefore fundamental to desire that it should constantly be detaching itself from its object and finding new representations. This property of desire, which is a normal aspect of conscious desire, becomes more pronounced—one might even say more frenzied—with repressed desires. Much of what I have said about castration is reminiscent of what Freud says about the behavior of desire in dreams, in neurotic symptoms (as well as in the "symptoms," such as slips-of-the-tongue and certain misreadings, which constitute "the psychopathology of everyday life"), and in art. Repressed desires seek to be "ex-pressed," but in order to be "pressed out," they must, so to speak, become "ex-centric" to themselves and avoid censorship by moving about among "innocent" images. Displacement is one of the principal strategies of unconscious desire. But we have been moving toward the view that displacement is crucial to a phenomenology of conscious *or* unconscious desire. To desire is to move to other places. And those places are representations—which is to say the images of fantasy.

But the floating of desire is a menace to coherent self-definition. Perhaps the principal strategy for stabilizing the self, both for individuals and for entire cultures, is to plot the immobilization of desire. On the cultural level, what we have usually called psychology is precisely an effort to arrest the movement of desire by creating a mythology of an inert human nature, governed by mental "faculties." The latter are abstractions, such as love and anger, which "correct" the continuous moving away of desire by providing totalities always fully present to our experience, always just "behind" our behavior as illuminating and unifying causes. The allegorization of desire, as Baudelaire himself illustrates, is a major sign of both a cultural and an individual repression of desire as *permanently displaced*.

"Le Beau navire" is a comparatively untroubled "reduction" of the woman's body to the juxtaposition of partial objects. We move from an abstract definition of a whole person's beauty ("Je veux te peindre ta beauté / Où l'enfance s'allie à la maturité") to the more concrete vision of a whole body in the second stanza; the praise of parts of the body begins in the first two verses of the third stanza, but it is momentarily arrested by the image of the majestic child in the last two verses of that stanza. The repetition of stanza one closes this tribute to totality, and we now proceed to a systematic survey of the woman as bits and pieces. The intensification of desire in the poem corresponds to visions of the woman's breasts, legs, and arms as phallic objects: detachable parts of the body which have a life of their own. The first stanza promises us a portrait of the woman's beauty, but it is her very seductiveness or desirability which ruins the possibility of a portrait. The progress of "Le Beau navire" documents the defeat of a willed clarity of intention ("Je veux te raconter . . .") by the fragmenting, floating affects which accompany the execution of that intention. The sign of desire's dominance is the end of unity and totality, and the transformation of the portrait into several portraits at once partial and mobile.

"Le Beau navire" also shows us that the detached phallic object is interchangeable with other objects. More precisely, we see an interchangeability of images in the poem which suggests the circulation of desire among various representations. In stanzas four and five, this circulation creates a certain incoherence. Different images get piled up as representations of the same object. Consequently, a linear narrative is interrupted by terms which are vastly different from one another but which are also repetitions of the same (breasts = armoire = shields, according to the energetics of desire), and the methodically executed painting announced in stanza one is abruptly destructured by the superimposing of various figures on one part of the painting. Composition is threatened by a proliferation of images which detach themselves from the composed body of the poem.[5]

"Le Beau navire" allows us to examine in the detail of a single poem the process by which the closed architec-

---

5. The dramatic discontinuity of the poem can of course be somewhat reduced by criticism. For example, J.-D. Hubert suggests a unifying logic in the images of stanzas five and six: the armoire resembles the hold of a ship (it is "full of good things") and becomes warlike through the etymological association with *armes*. Also, *panneaux* takes on a nautical meaning as the opening to the hold. Thus the "leap" from the boat to the armoires to the shields is reduced. (*L'Esthétique des "Fleurs du mal" | Essai sur l'ambiguité poétique* [Geneva, 1953] pp. 65–66). Nonetheless, in the poem the contrast persists between the linear continuity announced at the beginning and the anti-linear, anti-narrative accumulation of metaphoric equivalences in stanzas five and six. That is, an opposition between two modes of composing the woman's beauty (one of which, as we have seen, involves "de-composing" her presence) could be considered as a warning to criticism *not* to seek to establish the "rationality" of the poem's images. For by giving in to this temptation we erase the tension between a calculated narrative clarity and the fragmented syntax of desiring fantasy, a tension which, it seems to me, is itself the principal meaning of "Le Beau navire."

tural form of *Les Fleurs du mal* is undermined. I referred
in Chapter Two to a tension in Baudelaire's poetry
between a "secret architecture," in which the secrets
would be merely hidden beginnings and conclusions,
and another type of order, the logic of which would
involve the shattering of architectural orders. This tension is also an opposition between two types of meaning: that which lends itself to thematic formulations,
and another type definable perhaps only in terms of the
strategies which move toward (or retreat from) a destabilizing of sense. "Le Beau navire" is especially instructive about these conflicts. Indeed, the pedagogical
intent of the poem is realized less in a narrative or
pictorial account of the woman's beauty than in an
exemplary display of two sets of epistemological and
esthetic assumptions. The knowledge of the woman
promised in the first stanza turns out to be an impossible project; it is vulnerable to a kind of image-
producing machine which replaces the whole person
with scattered discontinuities. And the woman's
beauty travels far from her body; it is moved around
among the dislocating metaphors of a desiring imagination. This dislocation is a kind of violence—but it is
of course the violence of energetic metaphorical activity. There is, however, a certain compositional taming
of this violence in "Le Beau navire," a self-consciously

I might add that Hubert's book is the best stylistic study of *Les
Fleurs du mal* that I know. He argues, it's true, for a view of the
poems which is very different from mine: beauty would be a repudiation of movement, an immobilizing of the senses. At the
same time, Hubert is constantly showing how ambiguity tends
"to enrich the poem by giving it a polyphony of meanings" (p.
149)—to which I would add: an indeterminacy of meaning, a
mobility of meaning.

reasoned procedural order which at least hints at a fear of that violence as more consequential, or as more literal. The whole, ordered body of the poem resists the fragmenting effect of local metaphorical feasts. Baudelaire will have only to misinterpret the violence of a desiring consciousness in order to close his work to the dynamics of desire.

This is what almost happens in "Les Bijoux." A blasé man of the world is remembering an evening of erotic pleasure with a woman who, in deference to his tastes, had gone to bed with him wearing only her jewels. He recalls her trying out poses which charmed him by their mixture of innocence and lewdness. The woman's decorated and perfumed body passed, piece by piece, before her lover's "clear-sighted and serene gaze," and she succeeded in shattering the poet's calm, in dislodging his soul from the "crystal rock" where it had been settled in peaceful solitude. The clinking sounds and mobile reflections of the jewels initiate a process of metamorphosis aggravated by the woman's movements. The loved one is "broken up" into shifting, partial designs. But the visual fantasies of unanchored or scattered identity appear to raise the specter of a more literal violence. The final image of "Les Bijoux" is that of the woman's body being inundated with blood:

> —Et la lampe s'étant résignée à mourir,
> Comme le foyer seul illuminait la chambre,
> Chaque fois qu'il poussait un flamboyant soupir,
> Il inondait de sang cette peau couleur d'ambre![6]

6. And as the lamp had resigned itself to die, and the hearth alone lit up the room, each time it gave a fiery sigh it [covered with] blood that amber skin.

The sexual connotations of the lover's hallucination are obvious: the light from the fireplace is spasmodically "poured" on the woman's skin; it is as if each instance of spreading light were a bloody ejaculation. The violent metaphoricity of sexual fantasy has become a fantasy of sex as literal physical violence.

Is the myth of a unified, whole self necessary to prevent the violence evoked in the last stanza of "Les Bijoux"? That violence occurs immediately after the poet sees a "new design" on the woman's body, that of Antiope's hips joined to a young boy's torso. The androgynous object of desire may designate a sexual indefiniteness intrinsic to desire itself. Desire is *excessively available* to the world; that is, its appetites, generated in fantasy, exceed those which would presumably "belong" to a definite sexual identity. The prostituted self is an androgynous self; the poet, as the *Journaux intimes* suggest, is also a woman. Baudelaire's misogyny can be understood partly in terms of a panicky effort to reject the feminine side of his own sexual identity, and, more generally, to put an end to the psychic scattering or self-disseminations of desire. Baudelairean sadism is an attempt to stop the woman from moving, for her movements excite desires which may both endanger her and reduce the poet's identity to a kind of mobile fragmentariness. The loved one's stillness is a crucial sign of a major Baudelairean enterprise: that of immobilizing desire.

7
Desire and Death

Love leads to crime. More exactly, the *pleasures* of love lead to crime. In his remarkable essay on Wagner's *Tannhäuser,* Baudelaire presents this idea within the Christian framework of the "two postulations" in human nature. There is a pendulum-like movement in human experience between "two infinites, heaven and hell." Wagner dramatizes the inevitable duality of love, its constant movement between a redemptive, mystical love and a ferocious, sacrificial love, "as if barbarity were inevitably destined to take its place in the drama of love, and carnal pleasure led, according to an ineluctable Satanic logic, to the delights of crime" (1224).

What is the relation between pleasure and crime? We might begin by noting a dichotomy between two versions of sexual pleasure in Baudelaire. On the one hand, there is the pleasurable excitement of "La Chevelure," "Le Beau navire, and "Les Bijoux," an excitement linked, as we have seen, to psychic mobility. These poems have often been read in terms of an effort to escape from the supposed immediacy of desire. I have been arguing that, on the contrary, Baudelairean distancing from the object of desire in these erotic poems is *the sign of* excited desire, and it shatters epistemological securities and ontological boundaries. Baudelaire can have an exhilarated ex-

perience of desire as the noncentered floating of unanchored partial selves. But he has another scenario for
sex, one which can be seen as a reaction against the
self-displacements of desiring fantasy. This second
version of sex is most explicit in "Sonnet d'automne." The poet refuses to reveal to his mistress his
"infernal secret," his heart's "black legend written in
flame"; instead, he pleads for a passionless lovemaking:

> Je hais la passion et l'esprit me fait mal!
>
> Aimons-nous doucement. L'Amour dans sa guérite,
> Ténébreux, embusqué, bande son arc fatal.
> Je connais les engins de son vieil arsenal:
>
> Crime, horreur et folie![1]

Quiet sex, without the edge, the *pointe,* of passion:
Baudelaire aspires to an excitement that would be
somewhat identical to sleep (the woman in "Sonnet
d'automne" is a "Berceuse dont la main aux longs
sommeils m'invite"). And the agitations of desire
would be reduced to an irritation of the nerves; the
lover keeps an oppressively watchful sense of a sinister explosiveness just under his erotic somnolence.
There is a meteorological equivalent of this state in
Baudelaire. It is the misty autumnal sky of, for example, "Ciel brouillé" and "Chant d'automne," a sky
which transforms the sun from a single ball of sharp

---

1. I hate passion, and wit irks me.
Let us love each other gently. Love, in his watch-tower, darkling
and in ambush, is stretching his deadly bow. I know the weapons
of his old arsenal—crime, horror, and madness!

light into multitudinous rays of pale, diffused light (in "Sonnet d'automne," the "so white" and "so cold" Marguerite is, like the poet, an "autumnal sun"). This form of pleasure can run into the obstacle of a woman who, unlike Marguerite, will not "be silent" and "love quietly." This seems to be Baudelaire's complaint in "Sed non satiata," in which the poet begs the woman to lower her flame:

Je ne suis pas le Styx pour t'embrasser neuf fois,

Hélas! et je ne puis, Mégère libertine,
Pour briser ton courage et te mettre aux abois,
Dans l'enfer de ton lit devenir Proserpine![2]

Ultimately, there is perhaps only one escape from the "hell" of insatiable desire: the forced and permanent immobilizing of the desiring woman, that is, murder. The milder versions of this "solution" are Baudelaire's fascination with cold women and, on the esthetic level, his notion of beauty as "un rêve de pierre." In the short poem beginning "Je t'adore à l'égal de la voûte nocturne," the poet confesses to loving his "grande taciturne," his "bête implacable et cruelle," all the more because of her coldness, and even because she seems ironically to increase the distance between the poet and the "immensités bleues" of his beloved "voûte nocturne."[3] To describe sex

2. I am no Styx to embrace you ninefold, alas;
   and, O lecherous Megaera, I cannot, in order to break your courage and set you at bay, become Proserpine in the underworld of your bed.
3. This is, however, a singularly ambiguous poem. For example, is the poet addressing a woman or the moon in the first stanza?

with this cold and cruel woman, the poet compares himself to worms climbing on a corpse: "Je m'avance à l'attaque, et je grimpe aux assauts, / Comme après un cadavre un chœur de vermisseaux." Ultimate coldness is also the permanent stillness of death. Even more: the macabre image from *Je t'adore à l'égal de la voûte nocturne* suggests a complicated strategy involving the projection of a wished-for coldness so that it may be reincorporated. Simply to make love to a frigid woman is perhaps not a sufficient guarantee of immobilized desire; it would be better to *be* the frigid woman. And so Baudelaire is not only fascinated by the woman's corpselike coldness; it is as if he would also devour her deathly frigidity, as worms devour a corpse, in order to become one with it.[4]

To a certain extent, necrophilia is the Baudelairean erotic ideal; it is sex with an absolutely still partner who, at the extreme, may even be devoured. In his moments of retreat from the shifting designs which desire proposes to the poet–lover, Baudelaire thus aspires to a sexuality compatible with death. Crime in Baudelaire is in the service of a certain type of erotic pleasure; the most convincing form of evil in *Les Fleurs du mal* is one deriving from sexual needs. Now we only infer an act of violence from images of frigid, corpselike women; there are, however, a few poems in which the immobilizing attack itself is described. This

4. In another poem, the image of lovemaking as one corpse stretched out alongside another corpse is explicit: "Une nuit que j'étais près d'une affreuse juive, / Comme au long d'un cadavre un cadavre étendu." And in "Une Martyre," Baudelaire asks the dead woman in the painting which the poem claims to describe if her lover has satisfied his immense desire on her inert and docile body.

assault may not be physical; it can be sublimated into scenes in which the poet nastily reminds a happy, active woman of suffering and death. In "Une Charogne," the poet asks the woman he loves to remember the "charogne infâme" they had seen that morning in order to drive home the lesson that she too, "la reine des grâces," will one day be "semblable à cette ordure." The theme of "Une Charogne" is of course a cliché of love poetry; it loses some of its banality in Baudelaire in the context of the sadistic project we are considering. The cruelly detailed description of the dead animal's stinking carcass should be placed alongside other curiously insistent reminders of repugnant realities in *Les Fleurs du mal,* reminders forced on happy, energetic women: "Réversibilité" as well as "Confession," a less familiar poem which comes immediately after "Réversibilité," in which a woman referred to as a "riche et sonore instrument où ne vibre / Que la radieuse gaieté" confesses just once her horror of life, in a bizarre and plaintive voice which makes the poet think of "une enfant chétive, horrible, sombre, immonde."

Baudelaire's most explicit poem of sadistic sexuality is "A Celle qui est trop gaie."[5] The first four stanzas portray an attractive, joyous, lively, healthy woman. Then the poet remembers feeling, on days when he was dragging his "atony" through a beautiful garden, that the sun was beating on his chest "like irony" and that his oppressed heart was humiliated by the fresh greenness of spring. And he "punished" a flower for

5. The chief competitor in Baudelaire for this distinction would be "A une Madone."

Nature's "insolence." In the same way, the poet goes on, he would like to "chastise" the woman's "joyous flesh," and the poem ends on the fantasy of a brutal maiming of the "too gay" woman. The theme of punishing Nature or the woman for being happy when the poet is sad is only minimally interesting. More worthy of our attention are the differences between the punishment of Nature and the chastisement of the woman—differences which suggest that the analogy between the two merely provides a comparatively respectable way of explaining the wish to torture the woman.

The woman's punishment is immediately connected to sex: the poet would like to crawl silently, "like a coward," toward the "treasures" of the woman's body one night "Quand l'heure des voluptés sonne." And he would furtively go to her bed

> Pour châtier ta chair joyeuse,
> Pour meurtrir ton sein pardonné,
> Et faire à ton flanc étonné
> Une blessure large et creuse,
>
> Et, vertigineuse douceur!
> A travers ces lèvres nouvelles,
> Plus éclatantes et plus belles,
> T'infuser mon venin, ma soeur![6]

In "A Celle qui est trop gaie," we find pleasure *in* the crime designed to "chastise" the woman for her lively

---

6. in order to chastise your happy flesh, to bruise your pardoned breast and open in your astonished side a wide, deep wound, and—O blinding rapture—through those new lips, more vivid and more beautiful, infuse my poison into you, my sister.

movements. And the crime involves nothing less than a re-creation of sexuality. As punishment for the woman's joyous sensuality, the man invents a dizzyingly sweet sexuality on her ravaged body. This ecstatic punishment is a simulacrum of "normal" sex. The wound on the woman's side is a new (wide and hollow) sexual entrance not too far from the "real" one. And, unlike the mutilation of the flower in which Nature is punished for its insolent beauty, the woman's punishment, the poet claims, actually makes her body more beautiful: the "new lips" he has made (with what instrument?) are "plus éclatantes et plus belles." But finally, these lips are there in order to change sex into murder; the woman will die not from her wound, but from the poet's venomous sperm. The substitution of a gaping wound for the woman's genitals and the poisoning of the man's sperm are simultaneous fantasies.

Baudelaire's sadistic fantasy is, astonishingly, more easily recognizable as sex than the fantasies inspired by the women in "La Chevelure," "Le Beau navire" or "Les Bijoux." The simulacrum is closer to its model than the model is to itself. But in fact this may be the purpose of the simulacrum. The "trouble" with sexuality in "La Chevelure" and "Les Bijoux" is that it moves so far away from the sexual act. In "La Chevelure," this is not felt as a threat, but in the violence hinted at in "Les Bijoux" we see the possibility of a retreat from the dangerously mobile fantasies of sexual desire. The notion of violence itself is highly mobile and ambiguous. The violence of metaphorical discontinuity seems to "move" into a frighteningly real violence, but then real violence, in "A Celle qui est trop gaie," becomes a solution to the "violent" mobility of gaiety. It is also a solution to the crazy ontological leaps in stanzas four and five of "Le Beau navire," as well as to the potentially disorienting ways in which the woman is addressed (and identified) in "L'Invitation au voyage." Baudelaire now remakes the woman's (and his own) sex, and then engages in a *final* sexual act. The venomous ejaculation into the wound at the end of "A Celle qui est trop gaie" also kills the desiring imagination. Desire will no longer "travel," and neither will the poet's being. The poet's sadism is an act of spectacular single-mindedness. The woman's movements are stopped, the poet's desires are no longer scattered into various disguises, and the macabre simulacrum of sex is an unambiguous, non-diverted penetration into a new "genital" opening. The word "sister" which so incongruously ends the murderous fantasy of "A Celle qui est trop gaie" is itself a sadistic simulacrum of the same word in "L'Invitation au voyage." In the latter poem, it was merely one element in the shifting patterns of the woman's identities. In "A Celle qui est trop gaie," it is of course an ironic conclusion to the fantasy of violence, but it also expresses a finalization of the woman's identity as the poet's spiritual companion: like him, she is now filled with death.

In what sense is this murderous freezing of physical and psychic movement ecstatic? We should first note that while the entire fantasy at the end of "A Celle qui est trop gaie" may cause pleasure, the words "ver-tigineuse douceur" are associated not with the moment of inflicting the wound but rather with the poet's mortal ejaculation into the wound. The simulacrum of sexual penetration includes a simulacrum of ecstasy in sex, of an ecstasy which is both like pleasure in other poems and yet radically different from it. Two extremely dense, enigmatic, but highly suggestive passages from Freud may help us here: they are from "Instincts and Their Vicissitudes" (1915) and "The Economic Problem in Masochism" (1924).[7] In the 1915 essay, Freud uses sadism and masochism in order to illustrate transformations in the objects and aims of instincts. He begins with a three-step process. The first step, which is somewhat confusingly called "sadism," is "the exercise of violence or power upon some other person as object." In step two, both the object and the aim change: the impulse to master is turned upon the self and its aim also changes from active to passive. Finally, the instinct returns to an object in the world, but since its aim has become passive, another person "has to take over the role of the subject"—that is, the dominant role of step one. This last case, Freud points out, is what is usually called masochism. But he then goes on to make distinctions which profoundly modify the entire scheme just proposed. The conception of sadism is made more complicated, Freud suggests, by "the circumstance that this instinct, side by side with its general aim, (or perhaps, rather, within it) [neben seinem allgemeinen Ziel (vielleicht besser: innerhalb desselben)] seems to strive towards the accomplish-

7. Volumes 14 and 19, respectively, in *SE*. The passage discussed from "Instincts and Their Vicissitudes" is in *SE*, 14:127–29.

ment of a quite special aim—not only to humiliate and
master, but, in addition, to inflict pains."

How does this happen? The "sadistic" child of step
one is indifferent to causing pain; he wants only to
master the world (or one "object" in it: his mother).
Freud's answer, as Laplanche has seen, has the most
radical implications for the very notion of sexuality.[8]
Once the masochistic stage has been reached in the
three-step process, the instinctual aim may change
from that of being mastered to that of experiencing
pain. And this is possible because ". . . we have every
reason to believe that sensations of pain, like other
unpleasurable sensations, spill over into sexuality
[auf die Sexualerregung übergreifen] and produce a
pleasurable condition for the sake of which the subject
will even willingly experience the unpleasure of pain."
The usual notion of pleasure and pain would therefore
have to be revised and subordinated to a more inclu-
sive view of sexual pleasure as a component of all sensations which go beyond a certain threshold of intensity. One finds this position elsewhere in Freud. In
"The Economic Problem in Masochism," he refers to
a section of the *Three Essays on the Theory of Sexuality* in
which he "put forward the proposition that 'in the case
of a great number of internal processes sexual excitation arises as a concomitant effect, as soon as the intensity of those processes passes beyond certain quan-

8. See Laplanche's analysis of this passage from "Instincts and
Their Vicissitudes" in *Vie et mort en psychanalyse,* pp. 150–57. The
chapter "Agressivité et sado-masochisme" leads to some startling
conclusions concerning the relation between masochism and the
genesis of human sexuality.

titative limits.' Indeed, 'it may well be that nothing of considerable importance can occur in the organism without contributing some component to the excitation of the sexual instinct.' "9

Pleasure and pain continue to be different sensations, but, to a certain extent, they are both experienced as *sexual* pleasure when they are strong enough to shatter a certain stability or equilibrium of the self. The quantitative bias of Freud's argument may bother us; is there really a point on a psychic thermometer beyond which the "heat" of sensation enters into contact with sexual excitement? The crucial point to hold onto is the association of sexuality with the organism's experience of something excessive. Let's push the argument one step further and say that Freud may be moving toward the position that the pleasurable excitement of sexuality occurs when the body's normal range of sensation is exceeded and when the organization of the self is momentarily disturbed (deranged) by sensations somehow "beyond" those compatible with psychic organization. Sexuality would be that which is intolerable to the structured self.

This is, it seems to me, exactly what Baudelaire's love poetry illustrates. In "Le Beau navire" or "Les Bijoux," there is of course no way to measure the intensity of the sensations alluded to. The excitement of sexual desire in these poems is manifested as a movement of fantasy which profoundly disorients the desiring self. Or rather, the desiring self *is* a temporally, spatially, ontologically disoriented being, a scat-

9. *SE,* 19:163.

tered, partial self existing nowhere but in the movements of fantasy. And Baudelaire's poetry—like all
art—would help us to see the problematic nature of
any effort to dissociate sensation from fantasy. Freud,
in the passage just quoted, appears to be defining sexuality only in terms of a transgressed boundary of sensory intensity. But Freud himself invites us to be skeptical of sexuality on a purely somatic basis; no one,
after all, has taught us more about those processes by
which human sensations immediately "move into"
fantasies. The "quantitative limits" which have to be
passed in order to produce sexual excitement may be
measurable only in terms of the fantasy-signs of psychic deconstruction, indeterminacy, and mobility.

The instinctual change of aim which Freud men-
tions in "Instincts and Their Vicissitudes" has important consequences for sadism. "When once feeling
pains has become a masochistic aim, the sadistic aim of
causing pains can arise also, retrogressively; for while
these pains are being inflicted on other people, they are
enjoyed masochistically by the subject through his
identification of himself with the suffering object." As
Laplanche emphasizes, Freud's 1915 essay is a crucial
moment in the history of the contradictory stands he
took on the question of primary masochism—a moment which will be "repressed" until the appearance of
Beyond the Pleasure Principle in 1920. In "Instincts and
Their Vicissitudes," Freud begins by discussing a *nonsexual* process in which masochism is derived from
sadism. The masochism of step three is a return to the
sadistic object-relation of step one, but, because of the
change of aim in step two, the subject seeks to be mas-

tered by the other instead of mastering him. But, one page later, when we reach the passage quoted at the beginning of this paragraph, sadism has become secondary, a masochistic identification with the suffering object. We would seem, then, to have two quite different kinds of sadism existing simultaneously once the infliction of pain has become an instinctual aim: an "original," nonsexual sadism which seeks to master the world, and a derived, sexual sadism which is actually a pleasurable fantasy-identification with the intense (sexualized) pain of the victim. [10]

Around 1920, however, there is a major turning point in Freudian thought which, I think, encourages us to question the idea of a difference between these two types of sadism. The theory of the death instinct leads Freud to reject the idea of an original sadistic impulse independent of masochism. In "The Economic Problem in Masochism," Freud speaks of the libidinal life instincts attempting to make the death instincts harmless; they do this by directing our impulse to destroy toward objects in the external world, and this impulse "is then called the destructive instinct, the instinct for mastery, or the will to power." Thus step one in "Instincts and Their Vicissitudes" turns out to be, like the sexual sadism which is really a projected masochism, a derived sadism. The very distinction between sadism and masochism is blurred by this redefinition of both instincts in terms of projections and identifications within a single instinctual field—the

10. From here on, my discussion differs in important ways from Laplanche's analyses (especially the view I take of the relation between "nonsexual sadism" [step one] and primary masochism).

field in which the death instinct, under pressure from a life-preserving libido, moves between the self and the world. And Freud can write, with a sense of the difficulty of achieving terminological precision in such highly speculative thought: "If one is prepared to over-look a little inexactitude, it may be said that the death instinct which is operative in the organism—primal sadism—is identical with masochism."[11]

The sexualization of destructive instincts is also ex-plained in the light of the fate of the death instinct in "The Economic Problem in Masochism." In a passage quoted a couple of pages back, Freud refers to his pre-vious theory of sexual excitement arising partly as a result of any processes in the organism passing beyond a certain threshold of intensity. But this explanation is seen as inadequate; another view is offered "which, however, is not in contradiction with" the one just mentioned. This other explanation has to do with the work of the libido on the death instinct. Once this instinct has been directed to the world and become "the will to power," a portion of it "is placed directly in the service of the sexual function," and this is "sadism proper." Another part of the death instinct "remains inside the organism and, with the help of the accompanying sexual excitation . . . becomes libidi-nally bound there. It is in this position that we have to recognize the original, erotogenic masochism."[12]

How satisfactory is this explanation? In the new ver-sion of the processes outlined in "Instincts and Their Vicissitudes," the problematic nature of the relation

11. *SE*, 19:163–64.
12. *SE*, 19:163–64.

between nonsexual and sexual sadism or masochism is made particularly clear. Already in the 1915 essay, Freud has trouble describing the relation between the two. He can account for the sexualization of pain, but he cannot quite define the mode in which sexual sadism and will-to-power sadism coexist: the aim of inflicting pain is pursued "side by side with [sadism's] general aim (or perhaps, rather, within it)." In "The Economic Problem in Masochism," the notion of sexual excitement as being initiated by a certain excess within the organism is judged to be inadequate, but in its place we seem to have little more than the abstract assertions that "a portion" of the will to power "is placed directly in the service of the sexual function," and that "erotogenic masochism" is the instinct of destruction "libidinally bound" within the organism "with the help of the accompanying sexual excitation described above" (in the passage on the exceeding of "certain quantitative limits"). How far are we from the tautological claim that libido libidinizes? The problem that seems to be skirted is the precise sexual nature of libido (which is also the life fact), and *the relation between sexual exitement derived from the life instinct and sexual excitement as a possibility within the death instinct itself.*

"The Economic Problem in Masochism" is a search for the element of pleasure in the impulse to destroy. The essay is extremely dense, and in spite of an effort to contain the issues by breaking up masochism into three types (erotogenic, feminine, and moral), it also has an extraordinary speculative mobility. This mobility is all the more striking given the essay's single-minded intention, which Freud firmly states at the very beginning. He will investigate the relation between the pleasure principle and both the death instincts and the life instincts, an investigation made urgent by the "mystery" of masochism. Interestingly enough, Freud sees no mystery or danger in sadism, which would appear now to be definitively relegated to a secondary, derived status. The danger of masochism is its apparent capacity to paralyze the pleasure principle, the "watchman" not only of our mental life but of life itself. How, then, does pleasure get into pain? What is pleasure?

Freud first goes back to his old equivalence of pleasure with a lowering of tension; from the perspective of his recent metapsychological speculations, the pleasure principle "would be entirely in the service of the death instincts, whose aim is to conduct the restlessness of life into the stability of the inorganic state." But Freud calls this view an inadequate explanation of pleasure—although by the end of the essay he will have given it an astonishing reinforcement. Sexual excitement, Freud goes on to say, proves that an increase in tension can be pleasurable. (This is particularly interesting since Freud usually speaks of the "pleasure" of sex in terms which rather fit the end of sex: if pleasure is the reduction of stimulation, it occurs only after the orgasm. Therefore there must be a "qualitative" peculiarity in pleasure. "Perhaps," Freud speculates, "it is the rhythm, the temporal sequence of the changes [der zeitliche Ablauf in den Veränderungen], rises and falls in the quantity of stimulus. We do not know."[13]

13. *SE,* 19:160.

However, this suggestive line of thought is abandoned and Freud returns to the problem of masochistic pleasure. After a short (and unilluminating) passage on "feminine" masochism, we have the passage on the "primary erotogenic type" from which I've already quoted, and finally a section on "moral masochism." It is only with this last type that Freud defines a sexual pleasure which is an intrinsic part of masochism itself. The moral masochist's need to be punished is closely connected to the wish to have passive sexual relations with the father. But the need to be punished derives from an original *de*sexualization of the father—his introjection as conscience or the superego. "Conscience and morality have arisen through the overcoming, the desexualization, of the Oedipus complex; but through moral masochism morality becomes sexualized once more. . . ."[14] Freud's ingenious suggestion is that moral masochism is a way of renewing part of the sexual excitement of the Oedipus complex; the need to be punished *includes* the (fantasized) pleasure of having sex with the father. But in making moral masochism sexually intelligible, Freud illuminates only one manifestation of masochism in an individual's history: the manifestation connected to his Oedipal feelings, or, more exactly, to an aspect of the Oedipal fantasy-drama. If we wish to hold onto the notion of a primary masochism, the intelligibility of sexual excitement in moral masochism is not very helpful in explaining the pleasure in "the primary erotogenic type." And so we find ourselves back to the enigmatically abstract middle section of

14. *SE,* 19:169.

"The Economic Problem in Masochism," and to the explanation of the libido "meeting" the death instinct and seeking to make it harmless.

It is only by returning to the most radical version of the relation between pleasure and the death instinct that we can hope to find an explanation of the erotic nature of masochism (and, by derivation, of sadism). One of the difficulties—recognized by Freud himself—in the theory of a death instinct is that, in clinical experience, the impulse to destroy is almost always accompanied by a libidinous satisfaction. Thus we never see the death instinct in its "pure" form; as Freud writes in *Civilization and Its Discontents* (1930 [1929]), "the desire for destruction when it is directed *inwards* mostly eludes our perception . . . unless it is tinged with eroticism."[15] There is one way to explain this mysterious invisibility of the death instinct: we never see it in a nonerotic form because *it is always already* "tinged with eroticism." Freud's position in "The Economic Problem in Masochism" is that the death instinct plus a countervailing libido produces erotogenic masochism. Strictly speaking, then, the death instinct, according to Freud, is not primary masochism; it becomes masochism only when it is "libidinally bound" within the organism. But it's possible that the death instinct *is* erotogenic masochism. This would involve our embracing the suggestion from *Beyond the Pleasure Principle* that "the pleasure principle seems actually to serve the death instincts."[16]

15. *SE,* 21:120.
16. *SE,* 18:63.

Freud himself was reluctant to abandon the idea of an antagonism between the pleasure principle and the death instinct; and so, also in *Beyond the Pleasure Principle,* a "new" psychic force is baptized which, unlike the pleasure principle, would be entirely on the side of the death instinct. This is the Nirvana principle, by which the organism tends to suppress all stimulation and reduce the quantity of tension to zero. Freud's hesitations about the relation between pleasure and destruction are also reflected in his shifting definitions of the principle of constancy to which the pleasure principle is intimately linked. Sometimes "constancy" seems to involve a reduction of tensions to zero; at other times, it is a homeostatic force which tends to maintain the organism at a certain level of tension (and this may even require an increase rather than a decrease in tension at moments when it is necessary to reestablish an equilibrium between the organism and its environment).

"The Economic Problem in Masochism" provides important clues for an understanding of Freud's fundamental hesitation about the nature of the pleasure principle (which, we should remember, was called the "unpleasure principle" in his early work). The essay also suggests that the dualisms Freud continually adopts (and, most notably, the dualism of the life and death instincts) both express and disguise an intuition about the profoundly ambiguous nature of pleasure in desire. This ambiguity can perhaps be located in the *inseparability of desire from death.* We have seen at some length that the pleasures of the desiring imagination are in Baudelaire (and, I think, generally) linked to the mobility of fantasy. Desire "travels," moves from one representation to another. This movement is destructive in two ways. First of all, images are constantly being abandoned for other images; secondly, the entire movement is generated by the need to get rid of the irritating lack in desire, to replace the emptiness in even the most ecstatic fantasy by the (imaginary) plenitude of satisfaction. But the latter would be the end of movement, of the irritant of desire; it would be immobility, a nondesiring stillness like that of inorganic matter. In both instances, psychic unity is being shattered, but, it might be argued, in crucially different ways. The investing of multiple images with the affects of desire involves a scattering of the self; a radical indeterminacy of being is the result of a continual displacement of being. The self is always dying to its own centers. The activity of desiring is never merely an adequate response to stimuli; it produces, in fantasy, more "objects" of desire than the world could ever be shown to have been provided in any "real" past or present. But, simultaneously with this expansive movement, the self is also shattered by the movement toward *mere evacuation*. The productivity of fantasy may be only a fringe benefit of a more economical motive: the need to *stop* desire by finding adequate satisfactions. The fact that the very nature of desire is, so to speak, to propose excessively inadequate satisfactions is irrelevant to this implicit ideal of economy. Fantasy-satisfactions create new lacks, and therefore expand the field of desire itself; but the very phenomenon of desire is also a strategy designed to rid the organism of all needs.

In discussing Baudelaire's poetry, I have spoken of

sexuality in terms of destabilizing fantasies. Sexual excitement momentarily breaks down that structure of the self which enables us to "bind" both internal and external stimuli within a controlling and organizing subjective wholeness. This excitement is threatening precisely because it destroys such organization and control. But if the aim of these explosive energy crises is to rid the organism of destabilizing desire, we might postulate a sexuality exactly identical with the end of sexuality. This can be reformulated in terms of the following proposition: the sadism of step one in "Instincts and Their Vicissitudes" *is* the death instinct. Freud defines that sadism as the impulse to master the world. But primary masochism is a kind of sexually exciting self-mastery or self-immobilization; it is the ecstasy of the discharged impulse, of a dissipated desire. If we dismiss the pseudochronology of steps one, two, and three of the process described in Freud's 1915 essay, we could say that erotogenic masochism is always present in the "sadistic" desire to master the world, and, conversely, that the supposedly nonsexual desire for mastery is always present in the erotic pleasures of both sadism and masochism.[17] In its violent projects

17. The chronology is false because of the intersubjective nature of the entire fantasy process. In the wish to master the other, we immediately encounter a resistance which redirects the desire for mastery onto the self. It seems likely that we experience simultaneously the desire to control the other, the desire to control the self, the desire to be controlled by the other, the masochistic pleasure in being mastered, and the masochistic excitement of identifying with the other's suffering in our sadistic violence toward him. The different steps of a process must already be accomplished at the moment the process "begins"; the various representations along a line of fantasy are merely the spelling out of an intentionality sufficiently dense to inspire the articulations of a fantasy-drama.

toward the world, the self would also be shattered by the fantasized pleasure of its own annihilation; the wish to arrest the movements of others would include the pleasure of restless desire finally being totally evacuated. Freud, we remember, has difficulty putting two explanations of masochistic pleasure together: the explanation which appeals to quantitative limits being exceeded, and the notion of libido "binding" the death instinct within the organism. What I'm proposing is that the Freudian death instinct is a myth actually meant to account for the inherent sexuality of death— that is, for the profoundly exciting nature of the ulti- mate exceeding of quantitative limits in the absolute "discharge" of death.

Sexual pleasure leads to the pleasures of crime. We are now in a better position to appreciate the logic of Baudelaire's statement in his essay on *Tannhäuser*. The simulacrum of sex which the poet fantasizes at the end of "A Celle qui est trop gaie" is, as we have seen, a more literal version of sex than the erotic experience of "La Chevelure." Baudelaire replaces movements of fantasy away from the body with an imaginary movement toward the body. But gestures of real vio- lence are substituted for the poet's exotic voyage, with the implicit aim of reaching absolute immobility.[18] And the sado-masochistic ecstasy referred to at the end of "A Celle qui est trop gaie" is the ecstasy of a sexual

18. In the context of a wholly different argument, Jean-Pierre Richard notes the "moderating function" of cruelty in Baudelaire: far from being a frenetic movement, Baudelairean sadism seeks to eliminate excess, to reestablish a balance of power between people ("Profondeur de Baudelaire," in *Poésie et profondeur* [Paris: Seuil, 1955], p. 124).

plunge in which the poet shares his own death with the woman's maimed body. The poet's "vertigineuse douceur" is a sadistic derivation of Freud's primary erotogenic masochism; it is a dizzying transgression of limits which has no other end but its own explosive and fatal force.

The terror of motion in the apparently uncontrolled motions of sado-masochistic sexuality is betrayed—both in Baudelaire and Sade—by a fascination with corpses.[19] Violating a dead body is a kind of immobile sex. If all the movements of sexual desire are interpretive versions of the object of desire, the necrophiliac's movements are pseudomovements. Necrophilic excitement is desire's interpretation of death; but this means that the lack in necrophilic desire is death itself, and this desire seeks the satisfaction of its own end. Sexual desire in "Le Beau navire" and "Les Bijoux" produces images which, so to speak, are hooked onto the observed movements of the woman's body; but nothing productive "feeds" the necrophiliac's gaze, and the excited desire for an absolutely still body merely seeks to produce more death.

19. For an intelligent if limited discussion of Baudelaire's affinities with Sade see Georges Blin, *Le Sadisme de Baudelaire* (Paris, 1948). Psychoanalysis seems to me indispensable for an understanding of sadism, and Blin wrote his book before the French discovered Freud. To work out the logic of the idea in both Baudelaire and Sade that erotic pleasure leads to crime would, I think, be the surest way of defining what they have in common.

8
A Spectral Id

The pleasures of self-torture can be felt more directly. Baudelairean irony paralyzes desire. The most concise descriptions we have of the poet's ironic relation to himself are in "L'Irrémédiable" and "L'Héauton-timorouménos." The mode of self-knowledge and of self-judgment evoked in these poems can perhaps best be understood in the light of Freud's notion of the superego. In Freudian theory, the superego is constituted by the introjection of parental authority, and especially of parental interdictions.[1] These interdictions are inseparable from two other aspects of the superego: first of all, its nature as an idealized version of the parent, and secondly, its intellectual function as an observer of the self. This complex bundle of attributes is suggested by Baudelaire's ambivalent attitude toward "la conscience dans le Mal" at the end of "L'Irrémédiable."

1. For Freud, the superego is one of the consequences of the dissolving of the Oedipus complex. Other psychoanalytic theorists—most notably, Melanie Klein—place the emergence of a superego (or at least the internalizing of prohibitions) at a much earlier period in the child's life. Sandor Ferenczi points out that the child's sphincter control depends on his having assimilated certain "educational" precepts, and Klein postulates a particularly fierce superego formed by the infant's introjection of "good" and "bad" objects in the first year of life.

Tête-à-tête sombre et limpide
Qu'un coeur devenu son miroir!
Puits de Vérité, clair et noir,
Où tremble une étoile livide,

Un phare ironique, infernal,
Flambeau des grâces sataniques,
Soulagement et gloire uniques,
—La conscience dans le Mal![2]

Our moral consciousness is ironic and infernal, but it is also our only relief and glory. The "phare ironique" is at once ideal and demonic, and its apparently contradictory character also belongs to a superego which is simultaneously an idealization of the judging parent and a ferocious version of the parent's judgment. Freud suggests that the superego is energized by the id, that is, by desiring impulses in the unconscious. The emergence of an idealized instance of the personality would therefore legitimize instinctual forces which, however, the superego condemns.[3]

The complex genesis of the superego suggests that

2. What a sombre, lucid exchange [there is, in] a heart become its own mirror—a well of truth, clear though black, wherein trembles a livid star, an ironic, infernal beacon, a torch of satanic graces, [man's] sole relief and glory—consciousness in Evil.

3. Freud's various efforts to define the superego's characteristics are not entirely consistent with one another. In *The Ego and the Id* (1923), the superego and the ego ideal appear to be synonymous. In the *New Introductory Lectures on Psychoanalysis* (1933 [1932]), the superego is presented as a psychic structure which fulfills three distinct functions: self-knowledge, conscience and the formation of ideals (see *SE*, 22:66). Freud also writes in *The Ego and the Id* that the superego derives from the first object-cathexes of the id; "thus the super-ego is always close to the id and can act as its representative *vis-à-vis* the ego" (*SE*, 19:48–49).

it may be the disguised representative, in the post-
Oedipal personality, of the death instinct. The parental authority internalized in the superego is connected,
before the resolution of the Oedipus complex, with
instinctual renunciation. In the case of a little boy, for
example, the fantasized castrating father had de-
manded that the child renounce his desire for the
mother. "Fantasized" is crucial, for it would be mis-
leading to stop at a definition of the superego as the
internalization of parental authority. The father-judge
is already an internalized figure, a fantasy of the real
father.[4] What, then, is the exact difference between
the punishing father of Oedipal fantasies and a
superego which presumably indicates a successful *resolution* of Oedipal conflicts? The answer may be that
the superego doesn't internalize anything; rather, it is
the result of a process of self-differentiation which
borrows from the image of an already internalized
parent. To put Freudian and Baudelairean terms together, we could say that the superego is the id which
has become its own mirror. The fantasy parent-judge
may do little more than provide a moral justification
for the pleasure of self-destruction. In the superego,
primary erotogenic masochism becomes a cultural
and ethical imperative. The immense importance of
the Oedipus complex for the death instinct would be
that Oedipal fantasies present the death wish in the

4. In the *New Introductory Lectures on Psychoanalysis,* Freud associates the superego with a kind of closed circle of fantasies imitat-
ing other fantasy-formations: ". . . a child's super-ego is in fact
constructed on the model not of its parents but of its parents'
super-ego" (*SE,* 22:67).

form of a morally and socially necessary interdiction of desire. The father's law negates incestuous desire and forces the child out of the family circle and into the world. And Freud would have us think that by sublimating this parental threat, we do indeed become social creatures, with a built-in mechanism for the control of antisocial impulses. This may be true, but the idealized parent can also be used to condemn *all* desire and to lead the organism to death. For in the superego the id, separated from itself, finds pleasure in attacking itself. The obvious sadistic aspect of the superego perhaps hides a more profound masochism which becomes evident if we think of the superego as desire turned against itself. Thus we return to the equivalence, proposed in the last chapter, between "original" sadism (the wish to master the world) and the death instinct. The last four stanzas of "L'Héautontimorouménos" could be read as Baudelaire's lament over this equivalence. We will be looking at the structure of the entire poem in a moment; here is its most famous stanza:

> Je suis la plaie et le couteau!
> Je suis le soufflet et la joue!
> Je suis les membres et la roue,
> Et la victime et le bourreau![5]

Baudelaire calls the oneness of the torturer and the victim Irony, the word used to describe the torch of "la conscience dans le Mal" in "L'Irrémédiable." Both "L'Héautontimorouménos" and "L'Irrémédi-

---

5. I am both the wound and the knife, both the blow and the cheek, the limbs and the rack, the victim and the torturer.

able" are suggestive of the ambiguity in "ironic" self-distancing. On the one hand, irony seems to involve a painful cleavage of the psyche. Consciousness observes and knows Evil; there is a distance between the two. The poet thus seems to be arguing for the hopeless duality of our being. Even the distinction between smiles and an "eternal laugh" at the end of "L'Héautontimorouménos" works in this direction. In the essay "De L'Essence du rire," Baudelaire describes a smile as "something analogous to the wagging [balancement] of a dog's tail or a cat's purring." A smile expresses joy, which manifests oneness or wholeness of being; the satanic nature of laughter has to do with its being "the expression of a dual or contradictory sentiment; and that explains the convulsive nature of laughter" (984). Smiles are on the side of *bercement,* of an unbroken rhythm of being; laughter expresses the duality of human nature, its entrapment within the "two postulations."

On the other hand, the image of the self or the heart as its own mirror (an image used in both "L'Héautontimorouménos" and "L'Irrémédiable") appropriately suggests that Baudelairean irony creates an *illusion* of distance. In stanza six of "L'Irrémédiable," the phosphorescent eyes of viscous monsters make a "light" which is an intensification of the surrounding darkness. Visibility is the result of a greater blackness emerging from a lesser blackness.[6] In a similar way,

6. Un damné descendant sans lampe,
   Au bord d'un gouffre dont l'odeur
   Trahit l'humide profondeur,
   D'éternels escaliers sans rampe,

irony would be a lacerating separation of desire from itself, a kind of functional cleavage which involves no difference of substance. Implicitly, the entire dualistic position—God versus Satan, spirit versus flesh—is exposed as an effort to give plausibility to the very notion of dualism. The "two postulations," a notion crucial to the idealism of the early poems of *Les Fleurs du mal,* are actually functions of each other. The spiritual dignity celebrated in "Les Phares," for example, consists of nothing more than the articulation of the curses, the blasphemies, and the ecstasy which constitute our fallen state. In "L'Irrémédiable," Baudelaire significantly speaks of "la conscience *dans* le Mal": consciousness *in* evil, not *of* evil. A dualistic position such as Baudelaire's "two postulations"— or, more generally, the Christian opposition between God and Satan—obscures the field of real differences in human life by positing a pseudodifference as an irreducible antagonism.[7] Dualism provides an illusory protection against the dangers of sameness. In psychoanalytic terms, what Baudelaire calls spiritual-

---

Où veillent des monstres visqueux
Dont les larges yeux de phosphore
Font une nuit plus noire encore
Et ne rendent visibles qu'eux

a damned man, going lampless down the brink of a pit whose stench hints at its watery depths, descending endless, banisterless stairs where slimy monsters glare with great phosphorescent eyes that deepen the darkness of the night and make nought but themselves visible

7. Christianity, however, betrays a sense of the sameness of opposites: Satan's origins are in God, his fall is a plunge away from his own substance.

ity, or "the postulation toward God," may be simply
an attempt to disguise a self-destructive movement as
a conflict between two distinct or authentically independent powers. The description of Irony as a kind of
lacerating moral consciousness in "L'Héautontimorouménos" and "L'Irrémédiable" should make
us suspect that the objectifying of a regulatory moral
principle can serve to legitimize the death instinct, to
confer on self-torture the authority of a divinely inspired "postulation." "Je suis la plaie et le couteau!"
implies no clash of opposing forces; it is rather an assertion of the fundamental sameness of apparently
distinct impulses. Baudelairean irony is the shadow of
a difference. It is a spectral repetition of desire *as* its
own negation.

The superego, it might be said, is a spectral id. There
is, from the very beginning, something insubstantial
about the superego. Unlike the image of the father in
Oedipal fantasies, it is not a fantasy-version of a real
person; instead, it is an identification of a part of the self
with one of the self's fantasies. But the very insubstan-
tiality of the superego makes it an "ideal" instrument
for a particular kind of knowledge. By assigning to the
superego the double function of self-observation and
self-judgment, Freud suggests the indissolubility of
its moral and epistemological roles. We may speculate
that in fact the two roles are identical. The knowledge
for which the superego is responsible *is* negated desire.
It is desire both petrified and etherealized, desire without affect; it is, in a word, desire transformed into a
concept of itself.

Baudelaire suggests something very similar to this in the "Notes nouvelles sur Edgar Poe," where he discusses art entirely in terms of vertical correspondences. It is through art that we seek to escape from the imperfection of human life and grasp a "revealed paradise"; thanks to our "immortal instinct for the Beautiful," we see the earth as being in "correspondence" with Heaven ("une *correspondance* du Ciel"), and in art we catch a glimpse of "the splendors beyond the tomb." Baudelaire goes on to distinguish between the enthusiasm or the spiritual excitement ("un enthousiasme, une exitation d'âme") which expresses "human aspiration toward a superior Beauty" and "passion which is *the intoxication of the heart.* . . . For passion is *natural,* even too natural not to introduce an offensive, discordant tone into the realm of pure Beauty; it is too familiar and too violent not to scandalize the pure Desires, the gracious Melancholies, and the noble Despairs which inhabit the supernatural regions of Poetry."[8] This superficially trite passage implies that desire can be abolished simply by being capitalized. It is not replaced by anything different from itself; it is simply raised to an allegorical status.

Several things come together here. In the vertical leap, "Nature" is denied. But in the "ideal" region beyond Nature, we find Nature allegorized and categorized into "pure Desires," "gracious Melancholies" and "noble Despairs." We appear to have an oblique but astonishingly faithful description of processes

8. *Oeuvres complètes de Charles Baudelaire,* ed. Jacques Crépet, 19 vols. (Paris: Louis Conard, 1923–53), 17:xx–xxi.

which I've been associating with the superego. The id
is idealized into a superior mental faculty by placing an
interdiction on itself. And we have a form of self-
knowledge which, as it were, is identical to the gesture
which erases the small *d* of desire and in its place in-
scribes a capital *D*. Morally, Nature is ennobled by this
erasure: discordance is eliminated and replaced by a
"pure" and "noble" emptiness. The capitalization of
desire also has important esthetic consequences. There
is a richly elusive art of shifting tones and heterogeneous images which, as we have seen, corresponds to
desire's incessant mobility, to the "infinis bercements
du loisir embaumé." In such an art, abstraction, as
Baudelaire suggests in the passage from "Fusées" on
"the infinite and mysterious charm which lies in the
contemplation of a ship," is the generating of "curves
and imaginary figures" by the real movements of real
objects. It is the extension of the concrete into memory
and fantasy. But with the negation of desire, we have
an immobile and immobilizing type of abstraction.
Instead of initiating a process of endless substitutions
(desire's ceaseless "traveling" among different images), abstraction is now a transcendence of the desiring process itself. And we move toward an art of
allegory, toward a poetry of what Baudelaire calls in
"L'Irrémédiable" "clear emblems" and "perfect tableaux" (a poetry illustrated by the juxtaposed and sta-
tic representations of the first part of "L'Irrémédiable"
itself).

9
Questions of Order

Je te frapperai sans colère
Et sans haine, comme un boucher,
Comme Moïse le rocher!
Et je ferai de ta paupière,

Pour abreuver mon Saharah,
Jaillir les eaux de la souffrance.
Mon désir gonflé d'espérance
Sur tes pleurs salés nagera

Comme un vaisseau qui prend le large,
Et dans mon coeur qu'ils soûleront
Tes chers sanglots retentiront
Comme un tambour qui bat la charge!

Ne suis-je pas un faux accord
Dans la divine symphonie,
Grâce à la vorace Ironie
Qui me secoue et qui me mord?

Elle est dans ma voix, la criarde!
C'est tout mon sang, ce poison noir!
Je suis le sinistre miroir
Où la mégère se regarde!

Je suis la plaie et le couteau!
Je suis le soufflet et la joue!
Je suis les membres et la roue,
Et la victime et le bourreau!

Je suis de mon coeur le vampire,
—Un de ces grands abandonnés
Au rire éternel condamnés,
Et qui ne peuvent plus sourire![1]

"L'Héautontimorouménos" records a poignant moment of hesitation when the poet, lamenting his separation from himself, seeks to escape from an existence now saturated with irony and to find once again the cradling rhythms of desire for the other. The first three stanzas are an attempted solution to the anguishing predicament described in the last four stanzas. A calculated aggressiveness is meant to save the poet from the aridity of self-conscious irony. Logically, the second section of "L'Héautontimorouménos" belongs at the beginning of the poem; we have only to add an implicit causal conjunction to stanza four ("Car ne suis-je pas un faux accord . . .") to realize that the second part explains the first part.

1.   *Heautontimoroumenos*
I shall strike you without anger and without hate, like a butcher, as Moses struck the rock, and from your eyelids, to slake my Sahara's thirst, I shall make the waters of suffering gush forth. My desire, big with hope, will swim in your salt tears like a ship setting out to sea; while in my heart, elated by your weeping, your beloved sobs will reverberate like a drum sounding the attack.

Am I not a dissonant chord in the divine symphony, thanks to the insatiable irony that mauls and savages me? That spitfire is in my voice, all my blood has turned into her black poison; I am the sinister glass in which the shrew beholds herself.

I am both the wound and the knife, both the blow and the cheek, the limbs and the rack, the victim and the torturer. I am my own heart's vampire, one of the thoroughly abandoned, condemned to eternal laughter, but who can never smile again.

The question of stanza sequence becomes singularly complex if we consider "L'Héautontimorouménos" from the perspective of the sado-masochistic sequence proposed by Freud in "Instincts and Their Vicissitudes" and elaborated in the case he discusses in "A Child is Being Beaten" (1919). We find in Baudelaire's poem both the Freudian articulation of sado-masochism into distinct steps and a masochistic identification with the victim's suffering which exposes the entire process as a single psychic "moment." Stanza one appears to illustrate the first type of sadism in "Instincts and Their Vicissitudes." The poet dramatically announces that he will strike his mistress "without anger and without hate." There is no sexual excitement, and if we accept Freud's suggestion that such sadism becomes sexually exciting only when the aim of inflicting pain is present, we can say that this cold cruelty does not have pain as one of its goals. Rather, it is the expression of a wish to master the world, or, as we see in the next two stanzas, to make the woman alleviate the poet's anguish. But as soon as the poet begins to give his reasons for striking the woman, his sadism is, so to speak, liquefied, or affectively enriched. The woman's tears ("les eaux de la souffrance") will "water" the poet's "Sahara," and his desire, now filled with hope, "will swim" on her sobs like a boat setting out to sea. The poet wants to be intoxicated by his mistress's tears, and the sounds of her suffering will be like drums in his heart awakening him to new conquests. What has happened to transform the passionless striking of the first stanza into exalted movements of desire which Baudelaire describes in images reminiscent of the cradling rhythms of desire in the earlier erotic poems of *Les Fleurs du mal?*

To answer this question, we will have to consider a second rearrangement of the poem's stanzas. I suggested a moment ago that the self-torture evoked in the second part of the poem belongs at the beginning, for it explains why the poet wishes to strike the woman. But it can also be argued that the last four stanzas belong *between* the two descriptions of cruelty because only they explain the eroticizing of cruelty, its beneficent liquefaction. In "A Child is Being Beaten," Freud divides young female patients' fantasies of children being beaten into three distinct fantasy stages: 1) My father is beating the child; 2) I am being beaten by my father; and 3) Someone (either undetermined or a representative of the father, such as a teacher) is beating children. Stage three resembles stage one, but, Freud adds, ". . . the phantasy now has strong and unambiguous sexual excitement attached to it, and so provides a means for onanistic gratification." The only explanation of this change lies in stage two, in which the child's fantasy of being beaten "is accompanied by a high degree of pleasure." So, as in "Instincts and Their Vicissitudes," it is masochistic excitement which explains the sexualizing of the sadistic impulse. But in "Instincts," Freud is describing an ideal psychic progression; his model is a deduction from clinical experience, but it never refers to particular clinical experiences. In "A Child is Being Beaten," however, Freud considers the question of

whether or not the events represented in these fantasies actually occurred, and he makes the crucial
point that the second phase—"the most important
and the most momentous of all . . . has never had a
real existence. . . . It is a construction of analysis, but
it is no less a necessity on that account."[2] Masochistic
excitement would therefore be derived from an unconscious fantasy-event which transforms nonsexual
sadism into sexual sadism. We find something similar
in "L'Héautontimorouménos." The relation between
the poet's cruelty toward the woman and his cruelty
toward himself is presented in a significantly dis-
torted way. Structurally, his self-torture is relegated
to the second half of the poem; logically, it is the reason why he begins to torture the woman (in order to
end the inner drought created by "voracious Irony"),
but the effectiveness of the sadistic strategy can be
understood only if we read into the poet's self-torture
a sexual excitement absent from his description of it
and which explains the shift from an affectless sadism
to a sadistic desire bursting with hope.

Finally, however, it is possible to think of the middle
masochistic stage of "L'Héautontimorouménos" as
identical to the cold cruelty of the first stanza. The coldness announced in stanza one may express the fantasy
of an ideally peaceful violence. This leads us to a final
speculation concerning "original" sadism in Freud's
scheme of sado-masochism in "Instincts and Their
Vicissitudes." This sadism *seems* nonerotic precisely
because it translates the dream of a discharge of desir-

2. *SE*, 17:185. See Laplanche's discussion of "A Child is Being
Beaten" in *Vie et mort en psychanalyse*, pp. 165–73.

ing energy which would not shatter the self into producing more fantasies: rather, it would merely stop the
self and others. Affectless destructiveness (directed
either toward the self or toward others) would be a
representation of the *goal* of primary masochism,
which is death, a definitive physical and emotional
stillness.

The "place" of self-torture in "L'Héautontimorouménos" is, then, extremely ambiguous. "Voracious Irony" explains why the poet wishes to strike
the woman, but his ability to identify with her
suffering—an ability derived from the (inferred) pleasure of the poet's own suffering—invites us to place
his self-devouring irony "between" the sadism of
stanza one and the sadism of stanzas two and three.
Even if the death instinct aims to shatter the self beyond all possibility of being shattered, its manifestation as sado-masochism includes the experience of a
sexually exciting shattering of the self, the experience
of a psychic mobility which is the sign of the life of
desire. In "L'Héautontimorouménos," Baudelaire appears to be affirming the vitalizing potential of sadism
in stanzas two and three. Finally, however, the actual
order of the poem—which at first seemed "wrong" to
us—properly suggests the hopelessness of his effort.
The liberating rhythms evoked in the second and third
stanzas are locked in between two versions of essentially sterile violence. "L'Héautontimorouménos"
thus suggests the mobility of the death instinct itself.
The impulse to end the wild displacements of desire,
unable to realize the absolute discharge of death,
moves among different representations of violence:

self-torture, calculated cold cruelty toward the other, and an excited participation in the other's suffering. Now even the cradling movements of desiring fantasy are under the aegis of the death instinct. And, bizarrely enough, it is precisely at the moment when the other has become nothing more than a projection of the poet's own lost or maimed capacity to desire that he or she will be most intently looked at. The slightly insolent turning away from the other which nourished desire in "La Chevelure" or "Le Serpent qui danse" is replaced, in the "Tableaux parisiens" and the *Petits Poèmes en prose,* by a fascinated and frequently murderous attention.

10
Nightmares of Narcissism and Realism

The principal "character" of the "Tableaux parisiens" and the *Petits Poèmes en prose* is a narcissistic, hysterically sentimental, and frequently sadistic pedant. These are also Baudelaire's most "realistic" poems; many of them describe scenes from contemporary Parisian life, and there is very little exotic fantasy of the sort encountered in "L'Invitation au voyage" or "La Vie antérieure." What is the relation between realism and narcissism, and between violence and intellectuality?

The poet's relation to others is now one of appropriation. The "Tableaux parisiens" and the *Petits Poèmes en prose* record the narcissistic version of the prostituted self. The crucial texts on art as prostitution (in the *Journaux intimes,* the essay on Constantin Guys, and the *Petits Poèmes en prose)* probably all belong to the last decade of Baudelaire's life. And since the poems in prose seem to illustrate remarks from the *Journaux* and the Guys essay on the artist's promiscuous openness to the spectacle of external life, it's tempting to think of all these texts as variations on a single notion of art as prostitution. There is, however, a crucial difference between the penetration and congestion of the self by multiple forms of the external world (a phenomenon described in "Le Peintre de la vie moderne"), and the poet's effort to find himself repeated in the world. In the first case, the poet is invaded by, is even constituted by, irreducible difference; in the second case, differences are reduced to mirror reflections. The child who gluttonously takes in the world with an "oeil fixe et animalement extatique" is set afloat in a universe of alien forms. At the extreme, he would become a theatricalized self, a succession of scenes never totalized by a unifying (self-) consciousness. In a similar way, the artist-prostitute, as we saw in Chapter Two, becomes a richly problematic identity, a shattered ego available to the various partial (and even sexually indeterminate) selves celebrated in the shifting tones and modes of address of Baudelaire's erotic poetry. But in the avid narcissistic appropriation of the other, we have a false prostitution of the self. The poet's availability to scenes from the external world is enacted as a process of partly willed, partly rejected self-recognition or self-identification.

The little old women of Paris (in "Les Petites vieilles") "intoxicate" an observer whose "coeur multiplié" lives each of their imagined pasts:

Mais moi, moi qui de loin tendrement vous surveille,
L'oeil inquiet, fixé sur vos pas incertains,
Tout comme si j'étais votre père, ô merveille!
Je goûte à votre insu des plaisirs clandestins:

Je vois s'épanouir vos passions novices;
Sombres ou lumineux, je vis vos jours perdus;

Mon coeur multiplié jouit de tous vos vices!
Mon âme resplendit de toutes vos vertus![1]

The confrontation here is typical of the "Tableaux parisiens" and the *Petits Poèmes en prose*. The poet watches from a distance, with a fixed and troubled gaze, pathetic "débris d'humanité." On the one hand, "Les Petites vieilles" and "Les Sept vieillards" are much more realistically descriptive than "La Chevelure" or "Le Beau navire." The poet's attentive gaze does produce a picture, a fairly distinct tableau of Parisian life. But these realistic vignettes are frequently composed of the narrator's conjectures, or become dream-tableaux. What the poet "sees" and lives in "Les Petites vieilles" are his own fictions about the women's past lives. He makes little novels: in the second section of the poem, he imagines one of the women as plunged into misfortune by her country, another as the victim of her husband, and a third as a Madonna tortured by her child. That is, the bits and pieces of observed life in a big city provide the poet with an opportunity to put bits and pieces together, to reconstitute a coherent life from an isolated image. And he reconstitutes those lives *for himself:* it is as if the poet could become whole only by fabricating a wholeness outside himself.[2]

1. But I, who watch you tenderly from afar, with my uneasy eye fixed on your tottering steps, as though (what next!) I were your father—unknown to you I enjoy secret pleasures: I watch your untutored passions flower, and dark or bright, I relive your vanished days; my manifold heart delights in all your vices, and my soul resplends with all your virtues.
2. In the prose poem "Les Fenêtres," the poet invents histories for the people he glimpses through the windows of Parisian build-

The detached gaze which records these Parisian scenes is at the same time an intoxicated and a troubled gaze. In "Le Jeu," the poet describes the somber tableau which unfolded before his "oeil clairvoyant" in a dream one night. He dreamed of frantic poets and old courtesans in a decrepit and filthy gambling den; he saw the colorless lips, the toothless mouths, and the feverishly convulsed hands of gamblers risking their honor or even their lives with a desperate recklessness. But more interestingly, he saw himself

accoudé, froid, muet, enviant,

> Enviant de ces gens la passion tenace,
> De ces vieilles putains la funèbre gaieté,
> Et tous gaillardement trafiquant à ma face,
> L'un de son vieil honneur, l'autre de sa beauté![3]

But then, still in the dream, the poet became terrified of his own envy of these men "courant avec ferveur à l'abîme béant," who prefer pain to death and hell to nothingness. "Le Jeu" brings us close to the profound drama of both the "Tableaux parisiens" and the *Petits Poèmes en prose*. The poet is now a cold and silent observer transfixed by envy. And his envy is an ontological hunger. The poet aspires toward other existences; he sucks them into himself. Desire in "La Chevelure"

---

ings. He goes to bed at night proud of having lived and suffered in others; the truth of his "legends" is unimportant, for they help him to feel his own existence, to know what he is.

3. leaning there on my elbows, cold, speechless, and envying, yes, *envying* those people's intense passion, the old bawds' dismal sprightliness, and all of them as they cheerfully sold, under my very nose, one, his long-established honour, the other, her beauty.

was at once full and empty. The fantasy movements
initiated by the lack in desire are a partial satisfaction
of desire, a filling up of the emptiness. We also find
pleasurable fantasies in the poet's rapt observation of
the little old women, as well as in his envy of the
gamblers' "tenacious passion," but now the condition
for fantasy is that it be entirely performed as the reality of other lives. The poet continues to invent (he
dreams of passionate gamblers and concocts a past for
each little old woman), but his fantasies are, so to
speak, alienated from his consciousness. They come
back to him in the form of fascinating and intoxicating spectacles of otherness.

Baudelaire's tableaux of Parisian life are instructive
about the realistic imagination, and more specifically,
about the nineteenth-century realistic narrator's relation to his story. The ideal narrator of realistic fiction is
an absence; he reports, as Flaubert repeatedly said, on
nature "as it is," giving us both "le dessus et le des-
sous" of the tableau. But the most accurate metaphor
for this project, that of art as a mirror of reality, also
exposes its ambiguity. For what we discover in much
nineteenth-century fiction is indeed a mirror, but it is
displaced: instead of the artist's work having become a
mirror of the world, it is the world which the artist has
transformed into a mirror. The willed separation of the
author from the world he describes has the effect of
immobilizing the author's self in allegorized social
history. An impassive—or even better, wholly impersonal—narrator faces "blocks" of himself in the
world. The writer of realistic fiction has implicitly denied that he himself can be an instance of mobile desir-

ing fantasy. As a result, his affectivity is, so to speak, relocated in a world cluttered with things which the narrator has to describe in order to *see* his own existence. Objects fill up the realistic novel as memory objects clutter the poet's mind in Baudelaire's "Spleen" poem beginning "J'ai plus de souvenirs que si j'avais mille ans." In Balzac, to take the most striking case, a soul appears to be lost among objects, imprisoned in a world whose somber and fascinating presence might be described by the Balzacian narrator in terms similar to those used by Baudelaire in "Le Cygne" to evoke the heavy immobility of a city burdened with the poet's past:

> Paris change! mais rien dans ma mélancolie
> N'a bougé! palais neufs, échafaudages, blocs,
> Vieux faubourgs, tout pour moi devient allégorie,
> Et mes chers souvenirs sont plus lourds que des rocs.[4]

Realism curiously accommodates allegory. It is as if the self-effacement required by an esthetic of objectivity were in fact enacted as an attempt to reappropriate a self "lost" in the world. Realism formulates as esthetic doctrine a relation to the world which belongs to the Lacanian category of *l'Imaginaire*. In Jacques Lacan's psychoanalytic theory, our relation to the world is marked by the Imaginary when it is characterized by an effort to master the world through a process of narcissistic identification with it. The source of the

4. Paris is changing, but nought in my melancholy has moved. These new palaces and scaffoldings, blocks of stone, old suburbs—everything for me becomes an allegory, and my memories are heavier than any rocks.

Imaginary order (and of all later identificatory relations) is the "mirror stage" of infancy. According to Lacan, this stage occurs between the ages of six months and eighteen months; the infant, still physically helpless, anticipates his own future physical coordination and unity by an identification with the image of the other as a *total form*. This is equivalent to saying that the child's self is at first constituted *as* another; the human self is originally an alienated self. The principal effect of the mirror stage on intersubjectivity can be found in relations of aggressive tension in which the self exists only as another and the other is seen as an *alter ego*. For example, in erotic relationships dominated by the Imaginary, each lover will attempt to capture his own image in the other. The subject, as Lacan puts it, "fixes himself on an image which alienates him from himself," and what he calls his *moi* is the "organisation passionnelle" appropriated from the other. But the other resists this appropriation, and here Lacan's description of human relationships has analogies to Sartre's analysis (especially in *L'Etre et le néant*) of our efforts to make other people reflectors in which we would see ourselves as the objects we want to be. [5] The other is seen as withholding the self, and so the knowledge one has of him through one's efforts to appropri-

5. But Lacan reproaches the existentialists for understanding "existential negativity" only "within the limits of a self-sufficiency of consciousness." Consequently, existentialist philosophy encourages the illusion of the self's autonomy and neglects the *"fonction de méconnaissance"* which always characterizes the self's structures. See Lacan's "Le Stade du miroir comme formateur de la fonction du Je telle qu'elle nous est révélée dans l'expérience psychanalytique," in *Ecrits* (Paris: Seuil, 1966), p. 99.

ate oneself in him is a paranoid knowledge. Indeed, for Lacan the alienating nature of self-identification makes the perception of the self in the other a paranoid perception from the very beginning.[6] At the same time, the appropriated self is an ideal self: the infant (and later the adult, to the extent that his relations are lived in the Imaginary order) sees in the other a total form, a full or completed being, which he possesses by identifying with it.

As we can see, the constitution of the self as Lacan describes it resembles the constitution of a superego. The imaginary construct of the self in the "mirror stage" is already both an ideal and a persecutory self. (The persecutors of the paranoid patient Lacan studied in his 1932 doctoral thesis were identical to the images of her ego ideal.) Lacan has argued that this alienated self-perception prepares the way for that identification with the rival which accompanies the resolution of the Oedipus complex. The "identificatory reorganization of the subject" which is brought about by the "introjection of the *imago* of the parent of the same sex" is possible because it is preceded by "a primary identification [that of the "mirror stage"] which structures the subject as a rival of himself." To the extent that this Oedipal reorganization includes the forma-

6. Infantile aggressivity, Lacan emphasizes, can't be understood only as a playful exercise of physical strength. It manifests an attempt to *capture* the self in the other. But, as Lacan himself obscurely suggests in "L'Agressivité en psychanalyse" (in *Ecrits*), the paranoid and aggressive nature of the effort to appropriate a self in the other in infancy can probably be understood only if we refer to Melaine Klein's scenarios of violent fantasy dramas which characterize the infant's relation to his internalized "bad objects."

tion of (or a new preeminence for) a superego, we might question any sharp distinction between what Lacan has called primary or preparatory identification and the secondary identification which occurs only as part of a process of sublimation made possible by the Oedipal stage. That is, in the intrasubjective relation "which structures the subject as a rival of himself," we may have not simply a "preparation" for the "secondary" identification which resolves Oedipal tensions, but perhaps above all a *model for* the identification which presumably designates a resolution of rivalry. Both the ideality and the persecutory nature of the post-Oedipal superego have their analogies in the originally constituted self.[7]

In a sense, then, the formation of the superego *repeats* the constitution of the self. But self-appropriation was simultaneous with a separating from the self. Thus we return to my earlier suggestion concerning the superego: it is not so much a fantasy-identification

7. For Lacan, however, "it is through the Oedipal identification that the subject transcends the aggressivity which is an essential part of the original subjective individuation." But he also sees the persistence in adult moral life of the "narcissistic structure" of the "aggressive tension" which accompanies it. The question of the extent to which these tensions *belong* to post-Oedipal sublimations and to the post-Oedipal superego would deserve a separate discussion. I argue that they do indeed belong to this advanced stage of development in my chapter on Racine in *A Future for Astyanax*.

For Lacan's concept of the mirror stage, see "Le Stade du miroir comme formateur de la fonction du Je telle qu'elle nous est révélée dans l'expérience psychanalytique" and "L'Agressivité en psychanalyse." The quotes from Lacan on the last couple of pages come from the *Ecrits,* pp. 113, 99, 117, and 119.

with a parental figure as it is an alienating distancing of the self from itself. And if the Lacanian Imaginary identification of the self in the other is simultaneous with the formation of an ideal and persecutory self, then Melanie Klein is right to locate the appearance of a superego in infancy rather than at the much later moment when the child incorporates the Oedipal father. There would be no reason to discuss Kleinian theory as a grotesquely improbable fable (as most psychoanalysts do); for the formation of conscience may not require elaborate mental operations incompatible with infancy. Rather, if we juxtapose Klein's proposals with Lacan's view of self-creation through self-alienation in the *stade du miroir,* we come to the conclusion that is impossible to constitute a total self without creating the superego. A complete, unified, total self *is* an ideal, other self. It is a psychological myth which corresponds to the subjective experience of psychic division (and not totality): the division between desiring impulses and those same desiring impulses turned against their own mobility and seeking a final fatal discharge.[8]

However, Lacan insists that neither the subject nor intersubjectivity in general can be reduced to the order of the Imaginary. It is particularly important in analysis that the patient be led from the order of the Imagi-

8. The functions of the Freudian ego are of course much more complex, and also more life-serving, than these remarks suggest. The ego is involved in the economizing of energy, in the blocking of internal and external stimuli which might overwhelm consciousness, and in fulfilling this function it obviously protects the organism's life.

nary to that of the Symbolic, by which Lacan means a
preestablished order structured like a language and in
which the subject can "find himself" as a signifier
within a system of symbolic exchange in the human
community. The subject, it should be noted, is still
another, but he is no longer the Imaginary other constructed on the illusion of resemblance, on what
Lacan has called the "mimetic trap [le leurre mimé-
tique]."[9] Rather, the subject would now find himself alienated in a symbolic system which he shares
with others. That system structures the human unconscious, and communication with the other can now be
enacted through the shifting positions of signifiers in a
system of symbolic exchange. The self is still an appropriated self, but what is appropriated is language *as*
the other, and not an ideal but alienated *image* of an
individual self. (In the resolution of the Oedipus complex, this would involve moving from a specular
rivalry with the father, in which the child seeks to take
the father's *place,* to an assumption of the function of
the father and, most fundamentally, of the symbolic
father who, as Law, is that which makes possible all
symbolic operations.)

Lacan's notion of the symbolic is difficult, and these
few remarks are clearly not intended to do justice to
either its complexities or its ambiguities. I want simply
to point out that Lacan emphasizes an alternative to a
view of the subject as constituted by a narcissistic identification with the other. And I think that this alternative has interesting analogies with the mobility of the

9. "Le Séminaire sur 'La lettre volée'," in *Ecrits,* p. 30.

desiring imagination in Baudelaire. The erotic poems from *Les Fleurs du mal* examined in the first half of this study define the desiring subject in terms of his continuously changing representations. The poet communicates with the loved one not by trying to capture his image in her, but rather by implicating her in an image-producing process. And the images belong neither to the poet's self nor to the woman's self; instead, they define a community in which the constant substitution of one image for another is itself the activity of both the poet's and the woman's desires. The poet's desire for the woman is enacted as a process of exchange and substitution which characterizes the universally human process of desire's displacements.

I introduced the Lacanian order of the Imaginary in connection with remarks on realism. The relevance of Lacan's Imaginary order to realistic fiction can be argued from different points of view. First of all, there is the mode in which the projection of human feelings into landscapes and objects is enacted (a projection which, in Balzac, is so complete as to give to houses or streets the status of moral figures in an allegorical drama). We are meant to be aware of this projection not as an interpretative view of the world so intense as to result in a fusion of the passionately interpreting self and external reality but rather as an objective description by a dispassionate narrator. It is precisely such "objective" description which results in the anthropomorphic nature of the world in realistic fiction. The narrator becomes an alienated presence in the things he describes. In most realistic novels, the narrator is not a character in the story; he is an omniscient presence without a name, and he is characterized by his presentation of a world presumably distinct from him. The passion which informs the great descriptions of realistic fiction from Balzac to Zola and Proust is the passion of wishing to capture alien forms. The most extreme, anxiety-ridden version of this passion is the frantic attention which Marcel brings to the world in *A la Recherche du temps perdu*. And even in the case of Proust's narrator, who does play a central role in his story, there is no fully constituted *character* at the "point" from which the description proceeds. Narrative description in realistic fiction could even be thought of as an attempt to appropriate a character for the one psychologically empty or at least incomplete presence in the novel: the narrator.

We find something similar in the relation between the narrator and the hero. The paradigm of realistic fiction has usually been defined as a confrontation between an exceptional individual and an unexceptional social milieu. This is true enough, but the hero is also confronted by a sort of partial version of himself. This, again, is the narrator of realistic fiction, a presence at once infinitely fascinated by and infinitely mistrustful of the main object of his attention. Stendhal is the clearest case of a narrator whose alienated and ideal self is in the heroes of his fiction, but a similar relation exists between Balzac and Lucien de Rubempré, George Eliot and Dorothea Brook, Melville-Ishmael and Ahab. And in all these cases—although once again Stendhal provides the most striking model—the narrator's knowledge of his hero is deeply paranoid. He distrusts his alienated and ideal self, and in fact he very often ends by having him killed. But this should make us suspect that in the narrator we see the subject already playing the moral part of the ideal self's role. The roles and functions of the Imaginary order may be distributed in very complex fashion. If the hero is an ideal self, he also embodies the danger and guilt of desire and is therefore condemned by a conscience operating through the narrator's voice. The hero's death is realistically explained as the triumph of more or less prosaic history over idealism or overreaching ambition, but, in psychoanalytic terms, it is also intelligible as manifesting the narrator's paranoid terror of the self he would both passionately appropriate as an ideal and passionately reject as an instance of dangerously energetic desire.

Finally, the attempt to possess a total form is expressed in what might be called the compulsive intelligibility of realistic fiction. To a large extent, the totality which the narrator discovers in the world is a totality of sense. The narrator's ambivalent relation to his heroic *alter ego* is contained within the larger, and essentially more comfortable, relation between the narrator and a world he makes sense of. Realistic novelists usually judge nineteenth-century society with great severity. But even when they appear to be most somber about the moral viability of contemporary life, Dickens, Balzac, Stendhal, and George Eliot manage, at least partly, to redeem the society they condemn by the very coherence of their social analyses. The realistic novel, for all its apparent looseness, is an extremely tight and coherent structure: it encourages us to believe in the temporal myths of real beginnings and definitive endings, it portrays a world in which events always have a significance which can be articulated, and it encourages a view of the self as *organized* by dominant passions or faculties.

The straining toward coherent sense in realistic fiction works against the hero. As my remarks a moment ago suggested, the ideality of the hero is ambiguous. Not only is he victimized by the paranoid aspect of the Imaginary relationship; he also seems to be perceived as a *doubtful totality,* and therefore as a dangerous (if also desirable) alienated self. The hero in realistic fiction has a double function. He is an alienated ideal self whom the narrator seeks to appropriate, but he also appears to be the rejected (and yet fascinating) possibility of disruptive impulses which might resist being enclosed in any structured totality at all. The sense-making procedures of realistic narrative align the narrator on the side of orders—social, moral, psychological—which would, and usually do, expel the hero from the world of realistic fiction. The ordered significance of most realistic novels objectifies a dream of psychic completeness. A reliably meaningful world *becomes* the narrator as he creates that world (and himself) in descriptions through which he simultaneously projects and captures images of completed and coherent forms. [10]

Perhaps all relations to the world dominated by the order of the Imaginary are condemned to a nonproductive time, that is, to the time of exact repetition.

10. I discuss these ideas about realism at greater length, but without the aid of Lacanian categories, in chapter two of *A Future for Astyanax.*

The enterprise of constituting the self in the other and of transforming the other into an *alter ego* means that, ideally at any rate, all relations are perceived as relations between identical terms. And within the space which separates the subject from his own coveted image, time is experienced as a process of uncanny reoccurrences. In realistic fiction, this takes the form of characters' behavior merely manifesting what we already know about characters. Sartre's complaint about the "essentializing" of individuals in traditional fiction could be rephrased, in the terms being used here, as the unmasking of the writer's project of reducing the events of fiction to a parade of sameness. For example, it would not be wholly absurd to suggest that a Balzac novel becomes unnecessary as soon as its exposition is over. The entire work is already contained in the presentation of the work, and the characters merely repeat in dialogue and action what has already been established about them in narrative summaries. Their lives mirror the expository portraits made of them at the beginning of the novel.[11]

Baudelaire gives us a nightmarish version of exact repetition in "Les Sept vieillards," another poem from the "Tableaux parisiens" section of *Les Fleurs du mal*. The eery, spectral nature of a life dominated by the Imaginary is suggested from the very beginning. In the first stanza, the poet speaks of a city "pleine de rêves, / Où le spectre en plein jour raccroche le pas-

---

11. Georges Poulet speaks of Balzac's universe being reabsorbed in its Cause, of disappearing in the abstract Principle which already contains it. See *La Distance intérieure* (Paris: Plon, 1952), pp. 122–93.

sant." And those dreams consist of things looking like other things; they are theatrical imitations. The morning fog makes the houses seem taller than they are; as a result, "Les maisons . . . / Simulaient les deux quais d'une rivière accrue." The idea of simulation leads to an explicit reference to theater: the dirty yellow fog creats a "décor semblable à l'âme de l'acteur." It is in this theatricalized space that the poet, in the midst of a dialogue with himself ("discutant avec mon âme déjà lasse"), comes upon a miserably poor and wicked-looking old man, a creature so "broken" that his spine makes "a perfect right angle" with his legs. This Parisian tableau then becomes frankly hallucinatory: the poet sees seven versions of the same old man ("no trait distinguished" one from the other). He asks if he would have died from contemplating an eighth, "Sosie inexorable, ironique et fatal, / Dégoûtant Phénix, fils et père de lui-même." The poet doesn't recognize himself in these seven repetitions of the same, but it is nonetheless as if they were a theatrical representation of that separation of the self from itself which is the basis of specular self-identification. The allusions to theater in the poem are much more than a strategic preparation for an "unreal" scene. Together with the procession of the seven old men, these allusions remind us of the principal traits of imaginary self-identifications. There are also elements of persecution in the nightmare of "Les Sept vieillards." The old man's eyes are shining with "méchanceté," and the poet adds that he walked as if he were trampling on dead bodies, "Hostile à l'univers plutôt qu'indifférent." And, interestingly enough, the perhaps fatal eighth old man, whom the poet avoids by rushing home, is described as an "inexorable, ironic double." Even in "Les Sept vieillards," then, where the old men are not perceived as images of the poet, the process of an exact repetition of selves alienated from one another is connected to a cruelly "ironic" persecution.

Simulation in "Les Sept vieillards" is crucially different from the metaphorical activity of "La Chevelure" or "Le Beau navire." In both these latter poems, metaphor is the fantasy-repetition of a desired object. But it is repetition *as* difference. When the woman's hair becomes an aromatic forest and the waves which carry the poet away to an exotic land, or in "Le Beau navire," when the walking woman's breasts are seen as an armoire or a shield, these images both express a desire and provide substitutes for an "original" object of desire. They initiate a process of difference within repetition which illustrates the productivity of desire, the ingenuity with which it can be satisfied without an illusory appropriation of or identification with the other. In "Les Sept vieillards," Baudelaire suggests that ontologically tawdry actors inauthentically assert their identity with alien selves. And when the spectacle of an exact and impossible repetition takes place before his eyes, the poet panics; "exasperated" and "terrified," "sick" and "feverish," he rushes home and locks himself in. And his near madness resembles the "dancing" of an old sailing barge on a shoreless and chaotic sea, a dance strikingly different from the perfumed cradling movements of "La Chevelure":

Vainement ma raison voulait prendre la barre;
La Tempête en jouant déroutait ses efforts,
Et mon âme dansait, dansait, vieille gabarre
Sans mâts, sur une mer monstrueuse et sans bords![12]

12. My reason tried to take over, but in vain; its efforts were all
undone by the storm, and my soul danced and danced like some old
mastless barge on a monstrous, shoreless sea.

11
A Premature Foreclosure?

The process of alienating self-identification is even more explicit in the *Petits Poèmes en prose* than in the "Tableaux parisiens." In the poems in verse, Baudelaire's "coeur multiplié" lives the dramas of lives which he at least begins by recognizing as different from his own. His excitement comes precisely from his secret invasion of other existences, from his slipping into roles alien to him. In the *Petits Poèmes en prose,* appropriation takes the form of recognition. The person being watched is often already like the observing poet; the latter has only to confirm a sameness which the world conveniently represents for him.

There is a good deal of violence and cruelty in Baudelaire's prose poems. A prince compared to Nero has his friend the court jester killed in "Une Mort héroïque." The poet cruelly humiliates a glass-maker in "Le Mauvais vitrier," and he beats up an old beggar in "Assommons les pauvres!" In "La Corde," a child hangs himself; the "heroine" of "Mademoiselle Bistouri" is erotically stimulated only by doctors, and she dreams of a young intern coming to see her with his instrument case, wearing a blood-stained surgeon's smock. A man's savage irritation with the woman he lives with is dramatized in "La

Femme sauvage et la petite-maîtresse," "Le Galant tireur," and "Portraits de maîtresses." The poet is not unaware of all this cruelty, but we do have the impression of a certain distance from violence in the *Petits Poèmes en prose*. Bizarrely, the poet's worldliness is the result of his appearing to come upon these scenes from an entirely different world. The realistic images of Parisian life and the allegorical or even supernatural tableaux can get the same treatment, because the poet is an equally dispassionate observer of a city scene and of his own fantasies. Unlike the case in Balzac, the internalization of an object of description in Baudelaire's prose poems does not stylistically disrupt the description's tone and order. The world is appropriated as a theater for the poet's obsessions, but the poet nonetheless manages to remain a spectator, to be present only as an ironic consciousness. The psychic division which drew forth the laments and the exclamations of "L'Irrémédiable" and "L'Héautontimorouménos" is now the fundamental and unquestioned condition of Baudelaire's art; "voracious Irony" provides the narrative *comfort* of the *Petits Poèmes en prose*.

In his attempts to distinguish between neurosis and psychosis, Freud speaks of a defense mechanism "much more energetic and successful" than repression which would consist of the ego repudiating an unbearable representation and its affect and behaving as if this representation had never even reached the ego. This repudiation, unlike the repression of a sexual impulse, essentially involves the subject's relation with the external world. A reality distinct from the self is denied, and in the "Wolf Man" case, Freud moves toward the position that the crucial denial (*Verwerfung* is used here) is that of the absence of a penis in women. In his later work, Freud frequently uses the word *Verleugnung* to describe the repudiation of castration, which comes to be the prototype of all denials of reality. As Laplanche and Pontalis strikingly put it, there is, in symmetrical correspondence to neurotic repression, a psychotic repression *in* the external world (as if there were a "place" in reality where certain real facts could be hidden or, ideally, abolished).[1]

Much has been made of this Freudian line of thought in contemporary French psychoanalytic theory, and the most suggestive elaboration of Freud's idea is Lacan's notion of "foreclosure" *(la forclusion)*. Using as a point of departure Freud's ambiguity about whether the object of repudiation or denial is the perceived absence of a penis or an interpretation of that absence, Lacan makes of this denial a crisis of meaning. Freud had already said that the child's (and the psychotic's) repudiation of the woman's lack of a penis makes the subject unable to elaborate the infantile theory of castration. In Chapter Six, I argued for a view of castration as a model for the operation of meaning itself. Fantasies of actual castration can be interpreted as sexual representations of the detachable, movable nature of

---

1. *Vocabulaire de la psychanalyse*, p. 165. In Freud, see "The Neuro-Psychoses of Defence" (1894), *SE*, 3:58–60, and (in addition to the "Wolf Man" case), "Psycho-Analytic Notes on an Autobiographical Account of a Case of Paranoia (Dementia Paranoides)" (the case of Dr. Schreber, 1911), *SE*, 12:71; "Fetishism" (1927), *SE*, 21:152–57; and *An Outline of Psychoanalysis*, (1940 [1938]), *SE*, 23:201–4.

meaning itself. It is therefore necessary, to return to Lacan's argument, to symbolize castration. But this involves affirming it, introducing it into the self, making it represent the circulation of meaning which is the heart of symbolic thought. Instead, in *la forclusion* the child and the psychotic expel castration into "the real," by which Lacan means "an area which exists outside of symbolization"; they are engaged in "une abolition symbolique."[2]

Baudelaire's *Petits Poèmes en prose* can be read in the light of Freud's notions of *Verwerfung* and *Verleugnung* and Lacan's theory of *la forclusion*. I don't mean that Baudelaire was psychotic when he wrote these poems; he does, however, seem to have represented in them a psychotic relation to the world. Violence in the prose poems is simultaneously seen and repudiated.[3] There is not denial in the sense of a disappearance of perceived realities; nor is there any evidence that a sexual reality (the absence of a penis) or a sexual theory (of

2. "Réponse au commentaire de Jean Hippolite sur la 'Verneinung' de Freud," in *Ecrits,* pp. 388 and 386. In this essay, Lacan describes the phenomenon of *la forclusion,* but he is not yet using the word. See also "D'une question préliminaire à tout traitement possible de la psychose," in *Ecrits,* pp. 531–83.

3. What Freud called *Ichspaltung,* or splitting of the ego, allows for a recognition of what has been repudiated. As Freud wrote in *An Outline of Psychoanalysis:* "The problem of psychoses would be simple and perspicuous if the ego's detachment from reality could be carried through completely. But that seems to happen only rarely or perhaps never" (*SE,* 23:201). The simultaneity of seeing and denying would be the equivalent, in psychosis (and in fetishism, in connection with which Freud discussed the phenomenon in detail), of the simultaneous repression and return of the repressed in symptom-formation. In symptoms, the repressed is, in a sense, acknowledged.

castration) is being repudiated. Rather, the psychoanalytic reading I'm proposing has to be defended in more
general structural terms: in terms of the narrator's relation to the world, and more specifically, in terms of the
way in which he generates meaning from the incidents
he relates. In the *Petits Poèmes en prose,* there has been an
almost complete withdrawal of affect from the world.
It is as if certain fantasies had been projected onto the
world as a way of rejecting them. Freud did come to
make a distinction between *Projektion* and *Verwerfung.*
In his 1911 discussion of the case of Dr. Schreber, he
speaks of that which has been internally abolished
coming back to the subject from the world; and he
distinguishes this from the projection of a repressed
sensation onto the external world.[4] I think that the
difference may be verifiable only in the kind of knowledge which the subject has of the "repressed" material
in both cases. Projection is a frantic defense against the
return of dangerous images and sensations to the surfaces of consciousness; therefore, the individual ur-
gently needs to maintain that certain representations or
affects belong to the world and not to the self. In the
psychotic mechanism of *Verleugnung* or *Verwerfung,* on
the other hand, the split between the observing consciousness and certain threatening scenes has gone far
enough to allow for an almost scientific knowledge of
such scenes when they appear in the world. Divested
of any emotional urgency (whatever their content may
be), they can be dispassionately met and described as if
there were no *need* to describe them dispassionately as

4. *SE,* 12:71.

belonging to the world. That is, when the dangerous representations don't disappear entirely from the world, they (or disguised versions of them) "disappear" in the double sense that all emotional investments have been withdrawn from them and the only meaning they have for the interpreting consciousness is a more or less abstract, emblematic meaning.

In the *Petits Poèmes en prose,* the withdrawal of passionate and mobile significances from the world allows the Baudelairean narrator to respond to representations of his own violence with an appearance of objective, sophisticated interest. They are occasions for the display of narrative deftness as well as of a certain moral wit. But there are moments when this relation breaks down, moments of highly charged self-recognition. These outbursts of passion on the part of the narrator superficially designate a loss of sane rationality; they can also be read as signs of the poet's effort to *recover* sanity. Another passage from Freud describes such attempts at recovery. In the 1914 essay "On Narcissism: An Introduction," Freud wishes to explain the difference between the transference neuroses and schizophrenia or "paraphrenic affections." In obsessional neurosis and hysteria, Freud writes, the individual has retained his erotic relation to persons and things in fantasy. But the schizophrenic "seems really to have withdrawn his libido from people and things in the external world, without replacing them by others in phantasy." What happens to this libido? Freud's answer is that it returns to the ego in the form of a megalomania which then represents the mastering of this volume of libido, "and would thus be the counterpart of the introversion on to phantasies that is found in the transference neuroses." The failure of this narcissistic project results in hypochondria. As part of the paraphrenic's effort of recovery, ". . . the libido is once more attached to objects, after the manner of a hysteria . . . or of an obsessional neurosis. . . ." And Freud concludes with the remark that "the difference between the transference neuroses brought about in the case of this fresh kind of libidinal cathexis and the corresponding formations where the ego is normal should be able to afford us the deepest insight into the structure of our mental apparatus."⁵

Baudelaire's prose poems may provide us with an important clue to this difference. Freud describes a circuit in which libido is withdrawn from objects, invested in the ego, and attached once again ("after the manner of an hysteria") to objects in the world. It seems logical to suppose that when, in step three, the world is reinvested with libido, it will *resemble the ego.* The narcissism of step two will not be entirely abandoned; it reappears *as* a relation to the world. The clearest examples of this self-recognition are "Le Vieux saltimbanque" and "Une Mort héroïque"; more oblique versions of the same phenomenon can be found in "Chacun sa chimère," "Le Mauvais vitrier," "Les Fenêtres," the last anecdote of "Portraits de maî-tresses," "Laquelle est la vraie?" and, as we shall see, "Assommons les pauvres!" In the midst of the happy and noisy holiday crowd of "Le Vieux saltimbanque," the poet is fascinated by "a poor clown, bent, broken,

5. *SE,* 14:74 and 14:86–87.

decrepit, the ruin of a man." "Silent and immobile," the clown makes a dramatic contrast with the "joy, profit, debauchery" around him; he is "la misère absolue" in the midst of material security and "the frenetic explosion of vitality." As he watches the clown watch the crowd, the poet "felt my throat constricted by the frightful hand of hysteria, and it seemed to me that my eyes were offended by those stubborn tears which refuse to fall." And, "obsessed by this vision," attempting "to analyze my sudden pain," the poet says to himself: "I have just seen the image of the old man of letters who has survived the generation he so brilliantly amused; the old poet without friends, without family, without children, debased by his awful poverty and by the public's ingratitude, whose tent the forgetful world no longer wishes to enter."

The artist's victimization is even more shocking in "Une Mort héroïque." Fancioulle will die as a result of his prince's vengeful and sadistic capriciousness. Once again the poet is shaken by an image of the artist, especially of the artist's capacity not to see his own impending death thanks to the ecstasy of his creations. The narrator's "pen trembles," and tears come to his eyes as he tries to describe for the reader "that unforgettable evening." "Fancioulle proved to me, in a decisive, irrefutable manner, that, more than any other source of intoxication, Art has the power to spread a veil over the terrors of the abyss; that genius can play a role at the edge of the grave with a joy which prevents it from seeing the grave, for the artistic genius is lost in a paradise which excludes all ideas of death and destruction."

The passage from "Une Mort héroïque" brings us perilously close to the clichéd sentimentality of "Bé-nédiction" and "Elévation." But the *Petits Poèmes en prose* give us a much richer version of the mistreated poet. Now we have generalizations about Art or the Poet based on an encounter between the narrator-poet and a fantasy-image of himself. The *Petits Poèmes en prose* dramatize the self-splitting and the self-repudiation which, I think, provide the affective basis for Baudelaire's sentimental idealizing of the artist in the early poems of *Les Fleurs du mal*.

The identificatory scheme in the prose poems has changed somewhat from that of the "Tableaux pari-siens." In "Les Petites vieilles" and in "Le Jeu," the poet imagines himself as an emptiness which invents and assumes the forms of other lives; but he is also the horrified observer of lives destroyed by passions. That is, he is simultaneously the incomplete (and envious) self, and a superior, moralizing and yet fascinated ob-server of the disastrous effects of uncontrolled desires. The narrator, we might say, is like a superego suffering from the incompleteness which led to the creation of an ideal self in the first place; he has the worst of both worlds. In the *Petits Poèmes en prose,* the narrator's sen-timental identifications don't seem to include any envy for an affective coherence and unity. A unifying form has already been appropriated; we are now in the posi-tion of a fully organized cognitive and moral self which sympathizes with a self worn out by or de-stroyed in the midst of its passions (which are equated with the artist's inventive energies). The coordinated, unified self is no longer an alienated image; it has been internalized, and it provides the narrative point of view in the prose poems. There is still a self alienated in the world, but it is a broken desiring self. It is as if the superego were contemplating with melancholy fascination the very passions from which it has been derived. Baudelaire represents the persecutory instance of the self lamenting, at a distance, the fate of persecuted desire.

The organized self is the narrator who composes each one of the tightly controlled, perfectly unified anecdotes or moral meditations of the *Petits Poèmes en prose*. In his dedication to Arsène Houssaye, Baudelaire misleadingly emphasizes the fragmentary nature of his prose poems. Whereas he had insisted on the "compositional unity" of *Les Fleurs du mal,* he now invites the reader to stop reading wherever he wants, even to remove a "vertebra," for there is no "superfluous plot," and the two pieces of the writer's truncated, meandering fantasy will come back together again without any difficulty. "Chop [this fantasy] into numerous fragments, and you will see that each one can exist separately" (229). This can only mean that each *complete* prose poem could exist by itself. The *Petits Poèmes en prose* are a succession of small "total forms." Each piece is a perfectly rounded esthetic "jewel," an unbreakable whole which, however, doesn't necessarily belong anywhere in the structure of the entire volume. The book can be "truncated," but not the individual pieces. The importance of sequence in *Les Fleurs du mal* has to do with the poet's indecisiveness in that work: the way in which the poems of mobile desiring fantasy are placed tells us a good deal about the poet's willingness or refusal to be a permanently displaced self among the multiple representations of desire. A kind of structural prudence contains Baudelaire's erotic poems within the early poems of vertical transcendence and the later poems of immobilized desire (or of desire irremediably cut off from a condemning conscience). By the time of the *Petits Poèmes en prose*, Baudelaire's denial of the psychic mobility of his love poems seems definitive. Sequence is therefore no longer important, for in the prose poems the poet compulsively repeats a confrontation which has already taken place and which has meant the end of any affective mobility other than the immobilizing sadism of the superego.

But because the poet does recognize himself in the old clown and in Fancioulle, he cries when he sees the clown or tells the jester's story. Or rather, he both cries and repeats his murderous decision; several of the pieces in Baudelaire's *Petits Poèmes en prose* are ceremonies of sado-masochistic mourning. The poet is close to hysteria as he watches the old clown; he is "obsessed" by what he sees, and he tries to analyze his "sudden pain." The pain is his identification with the clown's suffering, but the poet's eyes are also "offended by those stubborn tears which refuse to fall." Is it the clown's suffering which offends the poet, or his refusal to show his suffering? If the poet *is* the clown, then his eyes, like the clown's, would be humiliated by the tears which would render his pain visible to a cruel public. Yet to the extent that the poet is also the persecuting public, he is sadistically offended by his victim's refusal to cry. But by crying himself, the poet makes reparation for his (and the public's) cruelty toward the artist. The artist-narrator's narcissistic pity for the old clown and Fancioulle partially makes up for society's insensitivity and the prince's murderous scheme. In "On Narcissism: An Introduction," Freud explains hypochondria as the failure of the megalomaniacal project. Pathological concern about the self would designate an inability to love the self, to reinvest libido narcissistically after it has been withdrawn from objects and persons in the world. Baudelaire's relation to the old clown and to Fancioulle is very much like this crippled form of self-love: the poet's fearful sympathy for the unhappy artist is hypochondria allegorized.

12
A Beggarly Ending

In my reading of the relation between the narrator and the persecuted artists or unhappy beggars of the "Tableaux parisiens" and the *Petits Poèmes en prose,* I am in general agreement with Charles Mauron's "psychocritical" interpretation of Baudelaire's later work.[1] Mauron distinguishes between a *moi créateur* and a *moi social.* The outcast, the prostitute, the actor, the clown, and the artist belong to the former category; the prince, the dandy, and the dispassionate narrator-spectator incarnate Baudelaire's *moi social.* For Mauron, the drama of Baudelaire's later work is the subordination of the writer's artistic self to his social self. Baudelaire punishes his own creative prostitution and moves toward a cold, sadistic "concentration" of his powers in figures hostile to the artist's self-dissipating energies. All aggressiveness is on the side of the prince-dandy (who represents the superego's harsh moralistic judgments of art); the *moi créateur* is the helpless victim of the condemnation of the *moi social.*

I think that Mauron is right to see Baudelaire, in the *Petits Poèmes en prose,* turning against his own creative energies; the cool narrator of the prose poems is the sign of a violent repudiation of Baudelaire's best

1. *Le Dernier Baudelaire* (Paris, 1966).

poetry. But *Le Dernier Baudelaire* is a thin work (especially if we compare it to other examples of Mauron's psychocriticism, particularly to his masterful *L'Inconscient dans l'oeuvre et la vie de Racine*). Its arguments are also vitiated by vague and trite oppositions between art and society, dependence and independence, aggression and poetry. When, for example, we consider the unanchored identity implicit in the fantasy-displacements of the poet's erotic desires, the meaninglessness of opposing dependence to independence should be evident, and the notion of a poetry of desire as devoid of aggression or violence is exposed as a conventional piety. Much of Mauron's vocabulary in *Le Dernier Baudelaire* belongs to a language the discrediting of which has been one of the achievements of psychoanalysis. Psychoanalytic theory has made the notion of fantasy so richly problematic that we should no longer be able to take for granted the distinction between art and life, or to feel that the word "creative" has any analytic value at all.

In an original and exciting essay on the *Petits Poèmes en prose,* Jeffrey Mehlman also objects to Mauron's neat dualism between life and art.[2] But Mehlman goes further: he sees in the prince-dandy figure a disruptive force which, like Mauron, I find alien to that figure's sadistic repudiation of (and narcissistic identification with) Baudelaire's images of maimed desire. For Mehlman, the prince-dandy affirms "a certain kind of metaphoricity (repetition–in–difference)"

2. "Baudelaire with Freud / Theory and Pain," *Diacritics,* Spring 1974, pp. 7–13.

which goes against a tradition of metaphysical idealism represented by the buffoon Fancioulle histrionically and "manically obliterating any awareness of death in his performed celebration of the mystery of life." Mauron falls into an idealistic trap: he conceives of the artist as bearing the burdens of higher values, of suffering "under the pressure of an oppressive—and falsely noble—weight." The fact that Fancioulle's art doesn't save him in "Une Mort héroïque" is to Mehlman the sign of Baudelaire's rejection of any "domesticating reappropriation," his refusal of dialectic's retrieval *(Aufhebung, récupération)* of difference or "alienated properties." Mehlman claims that the prince's genius lies in his "wrenching himself out of the dialectic through which he could only play master to Fancioulle's slave." The key element of the prince-dandy figure in Baudelaire would be "a metaphorical process which exceeds and traverses the dandy, disrupting any narcissistic idealization of self."

Unlike Mehlman, I find that metaphorical process not in the figures of the dandy or the prince, but rather in the fantasy-movements of Baudelaire's erotic poems in *Les Fleurs du mal*. The prince-dandy-narrator of the *Petits Poèmes en prose* is the death of metaphoricity; he is a pedantic, sadistic, and guiltily narcissistic immobilizer of desire. Consider, as a final example, a poem which Mehlman rightly sees as crucial for his argument: "Assommons les pauvres!" The narrator remembers having spent two weeks, sixteen or seventeen years before the writing of the poem, locked up in his room reading all the fashionable

books of the period which dealt with "the art of making people happy, wise, and rich, in twenty-four
hours." Dizzy and stupefied from having thus in-
dulged his "impassioned taste for bad books," the
thirsty narrator heads for a café with a sense of having
somewhere in his head "the idea of an idea, something infinitely vague" but nonetheless "superior to
all the old women's formulas" on which he had re-
cently gorged himself. But he meets a beggar who
holds out his hat to him "with one of those unforgettable looks which would overturn thrones, if spirit
could move matter, and if a mesmerist's eye could
ripen grapes." Inspired by his "good Demon" (who,
unlike Socrates' negative, prohibitive Demon, is "a
great affirmer . . . a Demon of action, a Demon of
combat"), he jumps on the beggar and practically
beats him to death after he hears the Demon whisper:
"Only he who can prove his equality is the equal of
another, and only he who knows how to win his liberty is worthy of it." While he is beating the
weakened old man with an enormous branch from a
tree, the "antique carcass" suddenly gets up, jumps
on the poet "with a look of hatred which struck me as
a *good omen,*" savagely knocks him around, and "with
the same tree branch, beat me to a pulp." The de-
lighted narrator ("Through my energetic medication,
I had thus given him back both pride and life"), indicates to the beggar that their "discussion" is over, announces that they are now equals, shares his purse
with him, and admonishes him "to apply to all your
colleagues, when they ask you for alms, the theory
which I have had the *pain* of trying out on your

back." The beggar, who has understood the theory, swears that he will take the poet's advice.

Mehlman interestingly juxtaposes "Assommons les pauvres!" with the Freudian "archeology of sadistic fantasy" in "Instincts and Their Vicissitudes" and "A Child is Being Beaten." Freud speaks, as we have seen, of an original nonsexual sadism which seeks to master or humiliate the object. But then he asserts the existence of another aim in sadism, which is to inflict pain. This second (and sexual) sadism is intelligible only as a result of a middle stage (separating the two forms of sadism from each other) in which the subject, having turned his instinct of mastery against himself, experiences the sexualizing of that instinct as a result of pain passing beyond a certain threshold of intensity. In the final stage of sadism, the subject masochistically enjoys the pain he inflicts on others. The specificity of this pain, as Mehlman puts it, "is to be oddly afloat between subject and object." The crucial masochistic stage is a turning away from the object to be mastered, but ". . . the loss of the object here is not enshrined *within* any interiority, but rather alienated . . . in the madly mobile displacements of unconscious fantasy." In "Assommons les pauvres!" the narrator begins by being in a position to dominate or humiliate the beggar; he ends by generating pain. And the Freud of "A Child is Being Beaten" authorizes us to construct the intermediary masochistic moment in which the object of consciousness is lost and pain is experienced as sexually pleasurable.[3] The

3. The Freudian passage in question is the one I summarize in my discussion of "L'Héautontimorouménos" (pp. 101–103).

narrator of "Assommons les pauvres!" reaches the
stage at which the subject masochistically enjoys the
pain he sadistically inflicts on others. Baudelairean
douleur in this prose poem (like masochistically exciting sadism in "Instincts and Their Vicissitudes")
would therefore be, according to Mehlman, somewhere "between" the poet and the beggar; it
wouldn't belong to either of them, but would be the
emblem of the irreducible difference between them.

In this reading, Baudelaire's prince-dandy becomes
a Nietzschean hero. Mehlman's ingenious application
to Baudelaire of Laplanche's reading of Freud
confirms his sense of the relevance to Baudelaire of
Gilles Deleuze's reading of Nietzsche.[4] The generation in "Assommons les pauvres!" of a *douleur* "afloat
between two subjects, inflicting its pain on the very
integrity of the subject," is also the generation of a
Nietzschean philosophy of meaning as a relationship
between different forces. Whereas Mauron sees the
dandy and the prince as obliterating the force or the
essence of the beggar and Fancioulle (and thereby attacking the *moi créateur),* Mehlman sees them as affirming a differential relationship against efforts by the
prostitute-histrion figure to negate differences or to
"retrieve" them dialectically. The persecuted clown
or artist or beggar would in fact be "the narcissist,
perpetually obliterating itself in (or as) the other,"
whereas the dandy "would insist as the perpetually
displaced instance of what Lacan has called *le symbolique."*

4. *Nietzsche et la philosophie* (Paris, 1962).

But what are we to make of all the disturbing signs of narcissistic appropriation of the other on the part of the narrator-dandy in "Assommons les pauvres!"? Mehlman neglects an important difference between the two poems he refers to most frequently: we have the reactions of both the prince and the narrator of "Une Mort héroïque" to Fancioulle, whereas the beggar of "Assommons les pauvres!" is confronted only by the narrator. The prince kills Fancioulle, and the narrator cries over him; in "Assommons les pauvres!" it is the narrator who, without crying, beats up the beggar. We have seen several cases of the narrator's imaginary appropriation of unhappy lives: in "Les Petites vieilles," "Le Jeu," "Le Vieux saltimbanque," and "Une Mort héroïque." I have called this fascination with the other a narcissistic pity for a maimed part of the narrator's self. And that part of the self is connected with both passions (in "Les Petites vieilles" and "Le Jeu") and art (in "Le Vieux saltimbanque" and "Une Mort héroïque"). The narrator's unsentimental reaction to the beggar in "Assommons les pauvres!" appears to break this pattern. But it does so by eliminating any possibility at all of mobility in the prince-dandy-narrator. The narrator's tears in "Une Mort héroïque" at least place him somewhere between the prince and the clown; they are signs of a failed effort at psychic recovery. Considered in the light of passages from Freud's 1924 essay on narcissism, the narrator's sentimental identifications with unhappy, persecuted figures in the "Tableaux parisiens" and the *Petits Poèmes en prose* dramatize his inability to love himself. Affect withdrawn from the world is unsuccessfully invested in the self, and when, as it were, the narrator comes across himself in the world, he finds a figure nearly destroyed by a cold, condemning world (which is similar to the narrator's own observing and moralistic superego). The narrator's narcissism in "Le Vieux saltimbanque" and "Une Mort héroïque" therefore includes some uncertainty about his being: it sets him afloat between the cool, ironic observer and the doomed poet-histrion. On the other hand, in "Assommons les pauvres!" any attempt whatever at psychic recovery is repudiated. The masochistic denial of the desiring (and potentially artistic) self is enacted as a brutal reduction of the other to the narrator's "argument." The narrator makes the beggar identical to him and thereby eliminates the difference between them.

In his seminar on Poe's "Purloined Letter," Lacan speaks of the minister as falling "into the trap of the typically imaginary situation" in his efforts to hide the letter he has stolen from the queen. And this trap is a "leurre mimétique": the minister imitates the strategy used by the queen, a strategy which he himself saw through. The queen had left the dangerous letter on the table, in full view of the king, who, however, had seen nothing. The minister had seen the queen feeling safe because she saw the king seeing nothing. She had not, however, seen the minister see *her,* and he had been able to pick up the letter and go off with it. With the police, the minister takes the same role the queen had taken with the king: he puts the letter in a highly visible place, rightly assuming that such a strategy would not enter into the police's notions of how a stolen letter might be hidden. But the minister also unwittingly repeats the queen's mistake. Like her, he sees that he is not being seen (by the police), but he fails to see, as Lacan puts it, "the real situation where he is seen not seeing." Poe's detective Dupin plays the same role with the minister that the minister had played with the queen, and as a result Dupin finds and steals the letter under the minister's nose. In referring to the minister, Lacan speaks not only of a "mimetic trap" but also of the "narcissistic relation" he is engaged in, and of his attempt to assume the impossible role of the "absolute master." The minister appropriates the queen's behavior as a strategy to win power. His exact imitation of the queen is designed to gain possession of the letter and mastery over her. He would narcissistically reduce her to his designs, and he also narcissistically assumes that no one will be astute enough to see him as he saw the queen (and this assumption is his stupidity). The minister imitates the queen in order to protect himself from the police, but keeping the letter from the police is of course the condition of the minister's power over the queen—so it is indeed true, as Lacan suggests, that the exact imitation of the other (the obliterating of differences) is equivalent, in Poe's story, to the narcissistic project of appropriating the other, of enjoying absolute power.[5]

Roles are reversed in "Assommons les pauvres!" but, as in Lacan's reading of Poe's story, imitation is initiated for the purposes of power. In the order of the Imaginary, the appeal of mimesis is its (deceptive)

5. "Le Séminaire sur 'La Lettre volée'," *Ecrits,* pp. 30–31, 33.

promise of making the world identical to the self. In beating up the beggar, the narrator *seems* to be defeating what Mehlman calls "an idealistic notion of social change" (we remember that the beggar had "one of those unforgettable looks which would overturn thrones, if spirit could move matter"). But why does the poet attack the beggar? He answers this question with the greatest clarity: it is to show him how "to win" his "liberty," how to "prove" that he is "the equal" of others. That is, the poet administers a lesson in independence, we might even say in autonomy. He teaches the beggar to be a master rather than a slave, but we never leave the terms and mode of the master-slave relationship. This relationship is enacted so literally as to be somewhat comical: the beggar is overwhelmed by a violent physical assault. And, wholly within the logic of narcissistic fantasy, the sign of the beggar's enslavement is his imitation of the poet. It is when he turns on the poet (who had regarded the beggar's "look of hatred" as a *"good omen"*) and begins to imitate him that his enslavement is consecrated. The poet's announcement: "Sir, you *are my equal*" should perhaps be read as "Sir, you are identical to me," or, even more radically, "You *are me.*" And the poem ends, most appropriately, with the beggar promising to repeat the poet's lesson with other beggars, who in turn will presumably repeat it with still others. Ideally, the poet's influence will spread everywhere; in numerous places and at numerous times, the world will mirror him. Far from being problematically afloat between the poet and the beggar, *douleur* in "Assommons les pauvres!" will merely be repeated (ad infinitum, were it possible) as a demonstration of narcissistic power.

The moment of pain is the moment of power, and also of pleasure. The substitution of *douleur* for *plaisir* at the end of the poem ("the theory which I have had the *pain* of trying out on your back") is by no means an elimination of the idea of pleasure. Indeed, the phrase is striking because when we read it we can't help but think of the absent word "pleasure." Pleasure has been crossed out and replaced by pain; but the pain reminds us of pleasure, which in fact is just "under" the pain. The poet's words to the beggar make us think of pleasure and pain at the same time: the pleasure we would have expected is expressed as pain. We are certainly reminded, as Mehlman says, of Freud's "archeology of sadistic fantasy." The pain is felt as the poet is trying out his theory on the old man's battered body, that is, even before the poet himself is beaten up. The sexual excitement of sadism lies in the sadist's masochistically enjoying pain, as Freud says, "through his identification of himself with the suffering object." In "Assommons les pauvres!" the poet's masochistic aim becomes literally evident, since he beats the beggar in order to make the beggar beat him. But—and this brings us back to my earlier discussion of a possible identity between the death instinct and the impulse to master the world—the purpose of psychic mobility here is the immobilizing of the self and of the other. The poet acts violently in order to initiate a violent action which will put an end to his own activity. We don't have the ontological indeterminacy designated by the poet's tears in "Le Vieux saltimbanque" and

"Une Mort héroïque," tears which threaten (though unsuccessfully) to close the gap between an ironic moralistic consciousness and Fancioulle's creative ecstasy. Rather, the ironic consciousness in "Assommons les pauvres!" transforms the beggar (who is structurally assimilable to the poet-histrion figure of other poems) into another ironic consciousness. If pain is at all afloat between the poet and the beggar, it is so that the beggar may become the poet and the poet may experience the destruction of the possibility of the beggar in himself. In other words, the experience of pain is set afloat so that the differences on which such floating depends may be abolished. Absolute power, ideal freedom, and a triumphant narcissism responsible for an epidemic of primary masochism: this is the complex lesson of "Assommons les pauvres!" The world, and not merely the poet, has become the "sinister mirror" in which the "shrew"—"voracious Irony"—watches herself set off an endless process of identical repetition.

There is, finally, an all-enveloping consciousness *of* repetition in "Assommons les pauvres!" (and in the *Petits Poèmes en prose* in general), a consciousness expressed in the Baudelairean narrator's ironic voice. When the poet sees the beggar's "antique carcass" getting ready for a counterattack, he cries, "Oh miracle! Oh the delight of the philosopher who verifies the excellence of his theory!" The status of thought is ambiguous in "Assommons les pauvres!" The narrator's discussion with the beggar is a mockery of "all the elucubrations of all those entrepreneurs of public happiness" whose theories had put him into "a state of mind approaching dizziness or stupefaction." (He gets in another dig at philosophy when he compares his active, affirmative Demon to "poor Socrates' . . . prohibiting Demon.") Countless books of social theory aren't worth the narrator's dramatically practical idea; the salvation of the poor can be accomplished at once—through philosophical thrashings. But this is of course too literal a reading of the poem. "Assommons les pauvres!" illustrates the narrator's ability to make fun of speculative theory, including his own philosophical inspiration. The poet is pleased by the success of his "demonstration," but the comic aspects in the description of his own behavior warn us not to take the denigration of bookish theories much more seriously than we take those theories themselves. The poet's demystification of abstract thought is now an elegantly ironic narrative act. And the concreteness of the lesson is somewhat dissipated in the emblematic nature of the tale.

More importantly, the poet's tone creates a certain distance between himself and the story he tells, a distance which partly protects him from our interpretation of his story. As in "L'Irrémédiable," irony is the poet's "torch of satanic graces," his "sole relief and glory." But in "Assommons les pauvres!" we have a more radical form of self-splitting than in either "L'Irrémédiable" or "L'Héautontimorouménos." On the one hand, the prose poem offers a remedy for what Baudelaire portrays elsewhere as the painful alienation of consciousness from passion. Not only is the difference between the narrator and the beggar negated; the success of the poet's lesson also depends on the beggar's understanding that the lesson is to be endlessly repeated. But then a new distance is created, one which separates the narrator at the moment of his narration from the very elimination of distance which is the subject of his tale. He becomes ironically conscious of the triumph of ironic consciousness. It is as if the superego were now moving away *from itself*. Its peculiar "relief and glory" may therefore lie not in the moral and self-reflexive functions which it is usually thought to exercise but rather in its capacity to repudiate its own aptitude for masochistic repudiations of desire. The successful realization of the psychotic design to stop all affective movements actually helps the poet to save himself from the success of his design. As a result of the death of desire, of the end of all affect, the poet is once again "on the move," even if only to add something humorously problematic to the end of affect.

But in this last example of Baudelairean mobility, we are of course very far from the ontological floating characteristic of the erotic poems in *Les Fleurs du mal*. Instead of the heterogeneous images and the psychic indeterminacy of "Le Beau navire" or "L'Invitation au voyage," we have in the *Petits Poèmes en prose* a kind of austere sophistication which consists in the poet's merely moving away from his own performances. His irony is equivalent to self-withdrawals; and this casual but devastating negativity would seem to be the poet's only escape from his violent projects toward his own desires. At the very limit of a suicidal enterprise designed to eliminate difference from the self's history, difference returns in "Assommons les pauvres!" in the form of ironic reservations about an act which abolishes difference. The sophistication which appears to save the poet is also fundamentally nihilistic. Of course there is no reason to think of the concluding chapters of this study as offering a central or final truth about Baudelaire. Indeed, we might best express our admiration for his achievement by returning to the cradling rhythms of *Les Fleurs du mal*. As a sign of our own reservations about a critical adventure which has, perhaps inevitably, enclosed the poet within an excessively coherent scheme, we can expose ourselves once again to Baudelaire's excitingly playful, if risky, adventure in self-scattering and self-displacement.

Index